ULTIMATE AIR FRYER COOKBOOK

Ultimate Air Fryer Cookbook

Your Essential Guide to Crispy, Juicy, Roasted Perfection

Jamie Yonash

Photography by Hélène Dujardin

ROCKRIDGE
PRESS

For general information on our other products and services or to obtain technical support, please contact our Customer Care Department within the United States at (866) 744-2665, or outside the United States at (510) 253-0500.

Rockridge Press publishes its books in a variety of electronic and print formats. Some content that appears in print may not be available in electronic books, and vice versa.

Interior and Cover Designer: Erin Yeung
Art Producer: Sara Feinstein
Editor: Anne Lowrey
Production Editor: Ruth Sakata Corley
Production Manager: Riley Hoffman

Photography © 2021 Hélène Dujardin. Food styling by Anna Hamptom. Author photo courtesy of Gabriel YoNash.

Hardcover ISBN: 978-1-63878-616-0
Paperback ISBN: 978-1-64876-744-9
eBook ISBN: 978-1-64876-745-6

R0

*For my parents, who prove each day of my life
that it is not shared blood that makes a family.
I love you more than you know.*

Contents

Introduction

There are days when I laugh out loud at the realization that I'm the author of two cookbooks. I'm not a chef. I do not love spending a lot of time in the kitchen. What I do love is sharing ways to make life simpler for busy families. The air fryer makes my time in the kitchen much easier, and that ease is the main inspiration for the recipes I create for my blog and my cookbooks.

One of the reasons the recipes on my blog have been successful is that I'm a lot like other busy parents. I want to put delicious food on the table for my family, but I don't want to spend all my time cooking. I don't spend time looking for recipes written by professional chefs. Instead, I prefer to find inspiration from real parents trying to feed their families food they will enjoy. Then I write recipes with the goal of finding ways to make our favorite dishes a little healthier in the easiest way possible.

The air fryer came on my radar about four years ago when I saw an infomercial. My husband wanted to get one immediately, but I was hesitant to add another small appliance that I might not use. We waited to see if this was a fly-by-night fad or actually a quality tool I would use for life.

I wish I had bought an air fryer sooner. The moment I started using it, I knew that buying it was the right decision. Just like with any new appliance, there was a learning curve, and every size and brand is a little different. I kept experimenting with mine, and it was worth the effort.

Now I can honestly say the air fryer is my most used small appliance. A few months after I purchased it, I tossed out my deep fryer because I knew I would never use it again. My air fryer is out on the counter every day at my house. It's busy cooking up meals several times a week and it's also handy for reheating foods quickly. I am 100% sold on the benefits of air frying. As you begin to use your air fryer, you will quickly see how easy it is to use. This appliance is for everyday life, and it deserves space on your kitchen counter!

Many air fryer cookbooks are available, and each one has its own pros and cons. I wanted to write a cookbook that shows everyday families the versatility of the air fryer. You can use this book to cook everything from breakfast to dessert. It really is the ultimate air fryer cookbook. You'll find recipes for basic staple air fryer recipes, but you'll also find unique recipes for foods you may never have considered cooking in the air fryer.

This cookbook has recipes for real people. You can find the ingredients at any grocery store. I have adapted some of the conventional recipes my family has been eating for years to be made in the air fryer, and they are even more excited about them now.

Get ready to learn all about air frying and its many benefits. Keep reading to find recipes that are simple, have a limited amount of ingredients, and do not require you to spend the whole evening in the kitchen.

Be sure to take a few minutes to read the beginning guide to air frying. It will lessen your need to experiment like I did. My tips and tricks will assist you with common questions and help you get the best results possible.

CHAPTER 1

Your Guide to Air Frying Perfection

You will find 150 recipes in this cookbook to help you on your air frying journey, including everything from steak to a Chocolate Lava Cake (page 223). It may be tempting to jump right into the recipes, but I encourage you to read this chapter, even if you've been experimenting with your air fryer for some time. Like many air frying cooks, the more I use my air fryer, the more I learn. You will likely gain some valuable nuggets of information from reading this chapter. Getting to know your air fryer, including how it works best and how to care for it, will help make your air frying experience even more enjoyable. With this knowledge and the recipes contained in this book, you will quickly move beyond using your air fryer to cook store-bought frozen foods and start making unique and delicious meals the whole family will love.

The Benefits of Using an Air Fryer

The air fryer was introduced in 2010 by the Phillips Electronic Company, which recognized that consumers had a desire for crispy foods but were concerned about the unhealthy cooking methods used to get those results. At that time, deep-frying and panfrying were the primary techniques used to get food crispy.

Since the air fryer was born, it has seen phenomenal growth and increasing popularity. In just a decade, this small countertop appliance has become a mainstay in kitchens around the world. Today there are many makes, models, sizes, and styles of air fryers available.

Air fryer technology allows you to cook foods using significantly less oil than deep-frying and produces even better results. Air fryers have a removable basket that doesn't have to be submerged in hot oil to get foods crispy. Instead, within the basket, the food sits on a crisper plate that has holes in it. The appliance circulates hot air around the food very quickly in a process called Rapid Air Technology, which exposes the food to heat on all sides. The heated air makes food crispy on the outside and the result is a delicious dish you don't have to feel guilty about eating.

Here are some more benefits of using an air fryer:

It's Healthy: The air fryer requires up to 80 percent less oil than traditional frying methods. Oil has 120 calories per tablespoon, and these calories add up quickly when food is deep-fried. You can save hundreds of calories by cooking traditionally deep-fried foods in the air fryer instead.

It Minimizes Mess: An air fryer keeps the cooking confined to the basket. There are no pans of oil to clean up. Many of the air fryer's removable components are dishwasher-friendly, or you can hand-wash them. To clean the outside of the air fryer, simply wipe it with a cloth.

It's Safer: Deep fryers and pans of oil on the stovetop pose safety risks. Hot oil splashes and can burn skin. The air fryer requires much less oil and removes the risks involved with using scalding oil.

It Increases the Crispy Quotient: The hot air rapidly circulating around the food in the air fryer basket usually results in a crispy texture. Foods that would normally require submersion in oil to get crispy need only a touch of oil in the air fryer to achieve the same great texture.

It Keeps Food Juicy: The air fryer is wonderful for searing meat to keep all the delicious flavors and juices inside. Adding a marinade or a light misting of extra-virgin olive oil to the meat helps the outside cook perfectly while the inside stays tender and juicy. Once you've cooked meat in the air fryer, you may never want to return to more traditional methods.

It Cuts Down on Cook Time: The air fryer uses Rapid Air Technology to quickly circulate heat within a compact space to allow for even cooking. Many recipes can be cooked at least 20 percent faster in the air fryer than in a traditional oven. The air fryer is also a great option for reheating and crisping up leftovers in only one to two minutes.

It Saves Space: The air fryer is a compact appliance. Whether you have a small or a large air fryer, it will fit nicely on the counter. It is the perfect appliance for small spaces like studio apartments, campers, and recreational vehicles. Take one on your next trip to add some variety to your vacation cooking. There is no need to survive on sandwiches and takeout when you can whip up an easy, delicious home-cooked meal in your air fryer.

It's Energy Efficient: The air fryer's compact size means it requires much less electricity than a conventional oven. Many foods cook faster in the air fryer, which also reduces energy consumption. This savings is especially helpful during the hot summer months, when electric bills are usually higher (not to mention, the air fryer will not heat up your entire kitchen the way an oven can).

It's Versatile: One of my favorite benefits of the air fryer is its versatility. Unlike other small kitchen appliances I own, the air fryer can cook a wide variety of foods. I can prepare everything from breakfast to bread in my air fryer; I can use it to roast vegetables, reheat leftovers, and whip up dessert. The options are endless.

Air Fryer 101

Air fryer technology is similar to convection cooking but takes place in a more compact space, which makes it more effective at crisping foods while also being more energy efficient. Air fryers use a cooking process called Rapid Air Technology, in which hot air rapidly circulates around the air fryer's cooking chamber. A heating element at the top of the air fryer radiates heat downward. As the heat is pushed downward, a powerful fan inside the appliance disperses hot air throughout the entire basket area. A crisper plate with holes in it sits in the bottom of the air fryer basket, allowing the rapidly circulating hot air to even reach the bottom of the food. The hot air removes moisture from the surface of the food, creating a deep-fried effect without using a large quantity of oil.

Types of Air Fryers

Since the invention of the air fryer, there has been an onslaught of new models and types on the market. There are pros and cons to each type. Your cooking habits and your needs will determine which style and size (and even color) you should buy. There are four main types of air fryers: basket fryer, paddle fryer, oven-style fryer, and air fryer lid. Read on to understand the unique qualities of each style and decide which is best for you.

BASKET FRYER

The original air fryer is a basket fryer. This type is the most common and comes in many styles and sizes. Its shape is similar to an egg and it is compact and easy to work with. Basket fryers can range in size from 2 quarts to 9 quarts. Most have a heating element above the basket. The basket has a handle and pulls out so you can easily check and shake the food, add food, remove food, and clean the basket. Basket fryers are simple and tend to have a longer life because they have fewer moving parts. Many include functions besides air frying, such as roasting, baking, and toasting. Many air fryers now have multiple presets for commonly cooked foods so you only have to push a button. All the recipes in this cookbook were tested in a basket fryer using the air fry setting.

PADDLE FRYER

The options for paddle fryers are more limited. A couple of different types are currently on the market. The paddle fryer is similar to the basket fryer, but it has a moving paddle inside that stirs the food while it's cooking. These machines tend to be wider and larger than basket fryers. Some paddle fryers have a removable paddle for stirring sauces or batters. The paddle fryer is a good choice for people who do not want to have to check on their food while it cooks.

OVEN-STYLE FRYER

The oven-style fryer is generally larger than the basket fryer and has a square or rectangular shape. It typically contains multiple racks and resembles a small countertop oven. The racks are usually dishwasher-safe, and you can take them in and out for ease of use. Oven-style fryers usually have a larger capacity that allows you to cook more food at the same time. They usually include a viewing window so you can see the food inside while it cooks. Oven-style fryers take up more counter space and are usually more expensive than basket fryers. You also cannot shake the food during cooking to redistribute it; instead, you may have to use a utensil, such as a fork, spoon, or tongs, to move the food around.

AIR FRYER LID

The air fryer lid is a specialized lid that works with an Instant Pot and turns the pressure cooker into an air fryer. The lid comes with an air frying basket that sits down in the pressure cooker to hold the food. There are multiple functions with the air fryer lid, such as air fry, roast, broil, bake, reheat, and dehydrate. The air fryer lid is not a stand-alone product and works only with the Instant Pot pressure cooker.

Sizes of Air Fryers

Air fryers are available in so many sizes that it can be difficult to decide which one will work best for you. Here is some information to help you narrow it down:

Small Air Fryers: Buying an air fryer with a 2- to 3-quart capacity makes sense if you are cooking for yourself or for two people. These models are smaller and take up less of your valuable counter space. They hold approximately six chicken wings at a time. This size is also great for reheating small amounts of leftovers. Smaller air fryers generally have a lower price point.

Medium Air Fryers: Families with three or four people will enjoy the convenience of an air fryer that has a 4- to 6-quart capacity. The basket holds more food, but the models are still on the smaller side. These air fryers will hold larger pieces of meat, making mealtime a breeze. Most 6-quart air fryers can hold a whole 4-pound chicken.

Large Air Fryers: Large air fryers in the 7- to 8-quart range will feed bigger groups of people and can cook large quantities of food at once, reducing the need to cook in batches. These models are perfect for big families. Many of the larger air fryer models have multiple functions and are handy all-in-one appliances. But remember: The larger the air fryer, the more counter space it will take up.

Extra-Large Air Fryers: Bigger and bigger air fryer models continue to be released. I see advertisements for air fryers as large as 9 to 12 quarts. Some are basket fryers and some are oven fryers. It is easier to use baking pans of different shapes and sizes in large units because there is more room inside. These units are exceptionally large, and the price goes up the larger the air fryer gets. These models may take longer to preheat and will use more electricity than smaller units.

NOT JUST FOR AIR FRYING

Did you know the air fryer also works better for cooking many foods you would normally prepare on the stovetop, on the grill, or even in the oven? People are often surprised to learn that the air fryer is more than just an alternative to deep-frying. There are endless options for foods to cook in the air fryer. Be prepared to think outside the deep-frying box as you get more comfortable using your air fryer. Before you know it, you will be using it to make many of your day-to-day meals.

Here are some examples of foods you can cook in the air fryer with wonderful results. This list may surprise you!

Hamburgers: Hamburgers (page 135) in the air fryer stay juicy while cooking quickly and evenly.

Steaks: Whether it's rib eye (page 141), sirloin (page 143), or T-bone (page 145), steaks cooked in the air fryer are juicy and flavorful and can easily be customized to each individual's preference.

Chicken tenderloin: You will love the results when you cook chicken in the air fryer. Wonderfully moist and flavorful, chicken tenderloins cooked in the air fryer will delight the whole family—with or without breading.

Vegetables: Cooking vegetables in the air fryer is quick and easy, which allows for fun and creativity without the stress.

Shrimp: If you keep a bag of peeled and deveined frozen shrimp on hand, you'll always have a few options for a healthy, delicious meal that will be ready in minutes.

French fries: Traditionally, making homemade French fries is a messy endeavor. Not with an air fryer! Air fried French fries (page 191) have never been easier, and the results are crispy perfection.

Dinner rolls: Keep your oven off and your kitchen cool by air frying your dinner rolls.

Quiche: Individual breakfast quiches (page 29) are a breeze in the air fryer. The finished product is irresistible and easy to customize for a spontaneous brunch or quick breakfast.

Pineapple: Air fried pineapple (such as the Honey-Lime Pineapple Skewers on page 215) is a sweet caramelized delight. You can "grill" many fruits in the air fryer for a tasty twist on a snack or a lovely addition to some of your favorite desserts.

Using Your Air Fryer

Air frying is easy once you get the hang of it. You'll find that you have more success if you take the time to learn how to use your specific model. It's also important to follow safety and cleaning instructions to prevent damage and injury and help your unit last longer. Follow these simple steps, and you will be an air frying expert in no time.

1. **Always read the manual that comes with your air fryer before using it.** Each air fryer brand has slightly different guidelines and suggestions that will improve your air frying experience. The manual will discuss important safeguards and precautions. Some recommendations to look for specifically include whether your air fryer basket is dishwasher-safe and if you need to preheat your air fryer.

2. **Read over the charts in your air fryer manual.** They will provide you with cook times and temperatures for common foods. These handy charts are specific to your particular make and model and will prevent inconsistencies in your cooking results.

3. **Remove the packaging.** If your air fryer is brand new, remove any packaging materials, film, or tape inside and outside the unit.

4. **Become familiar with your air fryer's display and control panel.** This panel may be digital or a dial, depending on your model. A basic panel will have time and temperature control settings. More enhanced panels may have presets for different types of food and different styles of cooking.

5. **Wash the air fryer basket.** Before you use the air fryer, it is imperative that you wash the basket in hot, soapy water. If your unit has a removable crisper plate, wash this, too. Rinse the items and dry them thoroughly. Do not use abrasive cleaners, steel wool, or scouring pads to clean the air fryer basket or the crisper plate. If you prefer to run the basket through the dishwasher, check your manual first to determine whether it's dishwasher-safe.

6. **Wipe down the unit.** Wipe the inside and outside of the air fryer unit with a damp, nonabrasive cloth.

7. **Position your air fryer in a safe place on your countertop.** Be sure the air intake and air outlet vents are not blocked while the air fryer is in use, which can cause the unit to overheat. Allow at least 4 inches of space around the back and sides of the air fryer and 4 inches of space above the air fryer for proper ventilation. Always keep your air fryer on a flat, level, heat-resistant surface.

8. **Insert the crisper plate and fryer basket and preheat your air fryer**, if **necessary.** When you are ready to cook with your air fryer, insert the crisper plate in the basket and slide the basket into the air fryer. Plug in the air fryer and turn it on. If your unit requires preheating (some do not), follow the manufacturer's instructions. The recipes in this cookbook have preheating instructions because most new air fryer models are set to automatically preheat unless the function is overridden.

9. **Set the timer.** All air fryers have a timer. Some models also have a setting you can use to remind you to check and turn the food halfway through the cook time. If your model does not have this function, you can always set a separate timer to help you remember. If you haven't already preheated your air fryer, set the temperature at this time. If your air fryer has different cooking functions, for the purposes of the recipes in this book, be sure to always select air fry, because all the recipes in these pages are made using the air fry function.

10. **Check the food.** Periodically check to make sure you are not overcooking your food, especially when you make a recipe for the first time. You can also open the drawer to shake, toss, turn, or adjust the food during cooking. The recipes in this book will let you know if any of these steps is required. Checking your food as it cooks is the single most important tip for good results.

11. **Use oven mitts or hot pads.** Remember that the air fryer basket will be extremely hot during and after use. Always use oven mitts or hot pads when handling the basket. Place the basket on a hot pad when it's out of the air fryer.

12. **Always use silicone-coated, wood, or nonabrasive utensils with the air fryer basket.** Many air fryer baskets have a nonstick surface that can be damaged by metal utensils.

13. **Never overturn the unit.** When cooking is complete, do not overturn the air fryer unit to get food out of the basket. Take the basket out of the unit or use heat-safe tongs to remove the food.

14. **Clean your unit safely.** If your air fryer basket has persistent food residue stuck inside, remove it from the unit and soak it in a sink filled with warm, soapy water. Do not use abrasive scrubbing pads on the basket or the crisper plate; they will create scratches on the nonstick surface. If the heating element of your air fryer gets dirty or has food particles on it, always unplug the appliance before you begin cleaning and make sure the heating element is no longer hot. Then clean the heating element using a small brush. NEVER soak or immerse the main air fryer unit in water! Keep the unit clean by wiping it down with a damp cloth. Always unplug the unit before wiping it down.

FIVE MOST COMMON QUESTIONS
ABOUT THE AIR FRYER

I am asked a lot of questions about air frying, and some I hear repeatedly. Learning the answers to these common questions will set you on the path to air frying success.

Do you need to preheat the air fryer?

Each air fryer model has its own specific recommendations for preheating. Always follow the manufacturer's guidelines. The recipes in this cookbook have instructions for preheating that you can skip if your air fryer does not recommend preheating. Remember that if you do not preheat the air fryer, you may need to add a few extra minutes of cook time to the recipe.

Can you air fry food that is frozen?

An array of foods can be air fried from a frozen state, and the air fryer is perfect for cooking many frozen convenience foods. Air fryer recipes will typically indicate specific cook times for frozen foods. A good estimate is to reduce the oven cook time on the package instructions by 20 to 25 percent when cooking in the air fryer.

Can you air fry without using any oil at all?

Yes. To get the best results, however, most foods and recipes require at least a light misting of oil. The amount of oil used is minimal and helps the food achieve a "fried" texture. Certain foods will not require any oil because they are naturally fattier and will crisp up on their own. Spraying a light coat of oil on foods is still much healthier than submerging foods in oil.

How do I keep food from sticking to my air fryer basket?

Spraying the basket lightly with oil will almost always prevent foods from sticking. A handful of foods are extra stubborn, and putting down a sheet of air fryer perforated parchment paper will take care of the problem. Feel free to spray a light coat of oil on top of the parchment paper for an even better result. Do not put the parchment paper in the air fryer without placing food on top of the paper. The paper is lightweight and will get pulled up into the heating element if it isn't weighed down.

How can I make my foods even crispier in the air fryer?

If your foods are not getting crispy enough, you can try a few tricks. The first step is to give the foods a light misting of oil at the beginning of the cook time and again halfway through the cook time. This step alone can make all the difference in the Crispy Quotient. You can also adjust cook times slightly; adding a few minutes can increase crispness. Finally, it is important to remember that not all types of food will get crispy. I have flagged some of these foods in the recipes so you have realistic expectations.

Useful Tools to Have

While using the air fryer is as simple as can be, some helpful tools and accessories will make preparing the recipes in this book even easier. Having these tools on hand has expanded the types of foods I can successfully cook in the air fryer and simplified the whole process.

Oil Spray Bottle or Mister: An oil spray bottle or mister is an essential tool for air frying. You can buy many different types at cooking supply stores or online. Never use aerosol cooking sprays, which can damage the air fryer basket's coating over time.

Parchment Liners: Parchment paper helps keep food from sticking to the crisper plate. Air fryer–specific liners are most convenient because holes in the parchment maintain the food's exposure to the hot air circulating underneath it. I find this parchment particularly useful when air frying seafood and certain vegetables. Packs of air fryer-specific perforated parchment paper are available in different sizes.

Heat-Resistant Tongs: Tongs are invaluable for flipping food while cooking and removing food at the end. Always use silicone-tipped tongs so the air fryer basket does not get scratched.

Bakeware: You can use any ovenproof pan in the air fryer. The key is finding bakeware that will fit inside your specific fryer basket. The simplest solution is to purchase an air fryer accessory kit that has bakeware specific to the size of your air fryer. This kit will allow you to cook a whole new assortment of recipes, like frittatas and casseroles.

Cooking Rack with Skewers: Kebabs will become a weekly menu item when you have a set of 6-inch metal skewers and a cooking rack that fits the air fryer. The raised rack allows total air circulation around the meat and vegetables, so you get the best results. Skewers make it easy to air fry seafood, chicken, beef, pork, vegetables, and even fruit.

Meat Thermometer: Food safety requires you have a meat thermometer on hand when cooking meat in the air fryer. It is especially important to cook meat to the proper internal temperature to avoid foodborne illnesses. There is no guesswork when you use a meat thermometer.

Silicone Muffin Cups: I use silicone muffin cups for recipes from muffins to meat loaf. They are safe for use in the air fryer and easy to clean. I can fit more silicone muffin cups in the basket than if I use a 6-cup muffin pan.

Silicone Basting Brush: Keeping a silicone basting brush handy makes it simple to baste and brush before and during cooking. Adding an extra coating of marinade while cooking gives the food that wow factor.

Silicone Egg Bites Mold: Many people have egg bites molds to use with their pressure cookers. They work just as well in the air fryer and allow you to cook scrumptious bite-size egg muffins in minutes.

Best Practices for the Best Results

The best way to get good results from your air fryer is to use it often. The more you cook in the air fryer, the more comfortable you will be and the better your food will turn out. But it can also be disheartening to spend a lot of your time in the kitchen troubleshooting. In this section, I'll help you save time by sharing my own experiences and experiments. Some of these troubleshooting tips are widely shared and a few I figured out by trying different methods over time.

Cut food into equal-size pieces: When a recipe requires you to slice, cut, or chop ingredients, make sure the pieces are the same size so the food cooks evenly, at the same rate, and ultimately tastes better. If food is not cut uniformly, the small pieces may end up overcooked and the large pieces might be undercooked.

Pat food dry: It is always a good idea to use a paper towel to pat your food dry before cooking, especially meats and vegetables. Removing the excess moisture prevents steaming and helps foods achieve a crispier exterior. This step takes only a moment but can make a huge difference in the taste and texture of the food.

Cut larger pieces of meat into several smaller pieces: Large pieces of meat can get overcooked on the outside before the inside is done. You can prevent this problem by cutting large pieces of meat into smaller portions. This step will ensure the meat cooks evenly and does not end up dry or tough. It is also a good option for small air fryer baskets that cannot hold one large piece of meat.

Cook most foods in a single layer: Cooking foods in a single layer ensures the air circulation around the food is optimal so all sides are evenly cooked and crisp. If you have a small air fryer, you may need to cook in batches to get the best results.

Avoid overfilling the basket: Overfilling the basket is a common mistake in air frying. When you do so, the air cannot circulate around all the pieces of food inside. The results will be dismal, with food that is cooked unevenly and more steamed than crisp.

Coat foods lightly with oil: Most foods will have a better result with a light coating of oil, which provides a better crunch, flavor, and color. Always use a non-aerosol oil spray or an oil spray bottle or mister. The additives in many aerosol cooking sprays can damage the nonstick coating of the air fryer basket and crisper plate. I fill my non-aerosol spray bottles with extra-virgin olive oil or avocado oil, both of which are wonderful for air frying. Never pour oil directly into the air fryer basket; instead, add it by spraying or tossing.

Turn or toss halfway through: You can never go wrong when you keep an eye on the food you are air frying. Shaking the basket midway through cooking or flipping food at the halfway mark will help foods cook evenly and get crispier.

Use a meat thermometer: I cannot stress enough how using a meat thermometer will help you get the best results from your air fried meats. Instead of wondering if the meat is completely cooked, you can simply check the internal temperature.

TROUBLESHOOTING YOUR AIR FRYER

PROBLEM	POSSIBLE CAUSE	SOLUTION
By the time my chicken nuggets are crispy, they're dried out inside.	The temperature setting may be too high.	Try cooking the nuggets at a lower temperature. Remember that the size of the nuggets will affect the cook time.
The air fryer is giving off white smoke.	The natural fat on the food could be cooking and producing grease, and the high temperature inside the air fryer may cause the grease to produce white smoke.	Add a few tablespoons of water to the air fryer basket before you start cooking foods high in natural fats, like bacon and beef, to help reduce the smoke.
Foods are not getting crispy.	The basket is overcrowded. The foods may have been too damp or wet. Certain foods will never crisp up in the air fryer.	Make sure you cook foods in a single layer when possible, and avoid overcrowding the basket. Pat wet foods dry before cooking. Spray the food lightly with oil to get a crisper result.
My food did not cook evenly.	Food may not have been turned or shaken during cooking.	Shake the basket or flip the food halfway through the cook time to achieve more even cooking.
The air fryer smells like burned plastic.	When the air fryer is heated the first few times, it may emit a plastic smell.	This smell should go away after a few uses. If it lingers, contact the manufacturer.
My food is stuck to the crisper plate.	The basket was not treated with oil prior to use.	Spray the basket with oil before adding food or use perforated parchment sheets made for air fryers.

The Recipes

Each recipe that ended up in this book was created, tested, and selected with care. I did research and invested time into getting each recipe just right because I wanted to include only recipes that were going to be amazing when cooked in the air fryer.

Even though my recipe selection process was rigorous, the scope of the book is far from narrow. The beauty of the air fryer is that it is incredibly versatile. Once you dive into the recipes, you'll be amazed at how many foods you can cook in the air fryer with great success.

This book includes recipes for breakfast, brunch, lunch, light meals, appetizers, poultry, meat, seafood, vegetables, desserts, and breads. You'll find many family-friendly recipes that will please even the pickiest eaters, as well as recipes for the solo cook and busy couples. You'll also find plenty of options for entertaining and even special occasions. There are classic crowd-pleasing appetizers like Loaded Potato Skins (page 89) and elegant Baked Raspberry Brie (page 71). All the classics are here, including Classic French Fries (page 191), Onion Rings (page 79), Breaded Calamari (page 170), Whole Roasted Chicken (page 111), Fish and Chips (page 167), Glazed Ham Steaks (page 23), Boneless Pork Chops (page 128), and Classic Hamburgers (page 135), as well as modern classics like Buttermilk Chicken Tenders (page 118), Veggie Burgers (page 203), and Twice-Baked Potatoes (page 192). You'll also find that the air fryer makes cooking dishes like Garlic and Herb Rack of Lamb (page 146), Maple-Glazed Duck Breast (page 124), and even Lobster Tails with Butter and Lemon (page 158) easier than you ever could have imagined. A large mix of main dishes and sides allows you pair recipes for informal and formal meals alike, and some recipes are full meals all on their own. There's something here for everyone!

But don't let the variety of recipes overwhelm you. Remember, my whole philosophy is centered around making cooking easy. As you browse through the pages, you will see that most of the recipes have 10 or fewer ingredients. These ingredients are all commonly available at any grocery store. Making meals in the air fryer does not have to be overly complicated or expensive.

In addition, each recipe has labels and tips. Labels include Gluten-Free, Dairy-Free, Vegan, and Vegetarian so you can quickly pick out recipes for different dietary needs. If you are crunched for time, look for the label 30 Minutes or Less, which indicates a recipe can be prepared and cooked in less than 30 minutes. Some recipes also include tips. Air frying tips provide shortcuts or helpful instructions for taking your air frying to the next level, and variation tips suggest alternative ingredients or methods that give you delicious options for the base recipe.

All the recipes in this book were tested in a large basket fryer. I have indicated the prep time and cook time for each one so you know exactly how much time it will take from start to finish. Remember that every air fryer is different. The particular brand, model, and size of an air fryer may change the cook time. I recommend watching the food closely during the last few minutes of cook time. If the food needs more time to cook, I usually add a few minutes to the timer but open the basket and check the food every minute or two because it can finish quickly! If the cook time is different than what is written in this book, make a note for future reference.

Now that you've learned all the air fryer basics, you're ready to make delicious food with your air fryer. Some great recipes to get started with include French Toast Sticks (page 31), Bagel Pizzas (page 60), Toasted Ravioli (page 72), Chicken Florentine Meatballs (page 101), and Mongolian Beef (page 133). But feel free to peruse the pages and find the recipes that appeal to your taste or sound fun to try.

Happy air frying!

ADAPTING RECIPES FOR HIGH ALTITUDES

Air fryers are still fairly new, and there is not a lot of research available on the changes needed for air frying at high altitudes. Moisture evaporates quickly at high elevations, which could cause foods to get overdone on the outside before the inside is done cooking.

Try making the recipes as written, but keep a close eye on the food. If it's overcooking, try decreasing the temperature setting 2 to 3 degrees per 1,000 feet of elevation.

The key is to always keep an eye on the food!

Now that you're all set up, let's start cooking, shall we?

CHAPTER 2

Breakfast and Brunch

Perfectly Crisp Bacon

Crispy bacon is a staple breakfast food with unparalleled flavor. The air fryer is a perfect way to produce delicious bacon, with a bonus: It's far less messy than stovetop cooking. All the extra fat and grease produced during cooking will drip down and collect under the crisper plate, which makes cleanup easy. Serve with a traditional breakfast of eggs, toast, and Sweet and Savory Breakfast Potatoes (page 21) or Seasoned Radish Hash Browns (page 33). And be sure to try the variation for added flavor.

DAIRY-FREE, GLUTEN-FREE, 30 MINUTES OR LESS

COOK TIME: 10 minutes
SERVES 4
TEMPERATURE: 350°F

8 slices bacon

1. Preheat the air fryer to 350°F.

2. Place the bacon in a single layer in the air fryer basket. (Air fry in batches, if necessary.)

3. Air fry for 5 minutes. Check the bacon for doneness and rearrange if it is no longer in a single layer. Air fry for an additional 3 to 5 minutes, or until crispy and lightly browned.

Air Frying Tip: Cooking bacon produces a lot of grease. If the air fryer is smoking, open it and carefully add a few tablespoons of water to the bottom. Remember that cook times will vary based on the thickness of the bacon.

Variation: Sprinkle some brown sugar on top of the bacon after you place it in the air fryer. It will give the bacon a caramelized flavor that is unbeatable. If you like spice, you can add a little cayenne pepper, too.

PER SERVING: Calories: 75; Total fat: 6g; Saturated fat: 2g; Cholesterol: 16mg; Sodium: 269mg; Carbohydrates: <1g; Fiber: 0g; Protein: 5g

Sweet and Savory Breakfast Potatoes

These potatoes are a filling and delicious side dish on any breakfast plate. Mixing white and sweet potato varieties adds a sweet and savory touch. This recipe pairs well with Green Chili and Cheese Egg Bites (page 22) and Perfectly Crisp Bacon (page 20). You can spice it up by adding a pinch of cayenne pepper to the seasonings in step 2.

DAIRY-FREE, GLUTEN-FREE, VEGAN

PREP TIME: 15 minutes
COOK TIME: 30 minutes
SERVES 4
TEMPERATURE: 400°F

2 medium russet potatoes, peeled and cut into ½-inch chunks

2 medium sweet potatoes, peeled and cut into ½-inch chunks

1 tablespoon extra-virgin olive oil, plus more for spraying

2 teaspoons minced garlic

2 teaspoons seasoned salt

½ teaspoon freshly ground black pepper

1. Preheat the air fryer to 400°F.

2. In a large bowl, combine the russet potatoes and sweet potatoes. Toss with the olive oil, the garlic, seasoned salt, and pepper.

3. Lightly spray the air fryer basket with oil. Place the seasoned potatoes in the basket.

4. Air fry for 25 to 30 minutes. Shake the basket every 5 to 10 minutes and lightly spray the potatoes with oil. Cook until nicely browned and slightly crisp.

Air Frying Tip: Cut the potatoes into equal-size chunks to ensure even cooking. If you like extra crispy potatoes, spray them with more oil while cooking.

Variation: Try replacing the seasoned salt with ½ tablespoon of Italian seasoning plus ½ teaspoon of salt for a fun twist.

PER SERVING: Calories: 175; Total fat: 4g; Saturated fat: 1g; Cholesterol: 0mg; Sodium: 725mg; Carbohydrates: 33g; Fiber: 3g; Protein: 3g

Green Chili and Cheese Egg Bites

Cheesy egg bites make for a light and fluffy bite-size breakfast or brunch food. They are so easy to customize with your favorite cheeses and spices, so feel free to experiment with the ingredients. I love using mozzarella cheese instead of pepper Jack and adding ¼ teaspoon of Cajun seasoning for a fun change.

GLUTEN-FREE, VEGETARIAN, 30 MINUTES OR LESS

PREP TIME: 10 minutes
COOK TIME: 10 minutes
SERVES 4
TEMPERATURE: 350°F

Extra-virgin olive oil, for the molds
5 large eggs
2 tablespoons milk
½ cup shredded pepper Jack cheese
1 (4-ounce) can diced green chiles, drained
¼ teaspoon salt
⅛ teaspoon freshly ground black pepper

1. Preheat the air fryer to 350°F. Lightly spray a silicone egg bites mold with oil.

2. In a medium bowl, whisk together the eggs and milk. Stir in the cheese, green chiles, salt, and pepper.

3. Pour 1 tablespoon of the egg mixture into each section of the egg mold until they are about half full. Carefully place the egg mold in the air fryer basket.

4. Air fry for 8 to 10 minutes, or until the tops are lightly browned and the egg is set.

Air Frying Tip: This recipe will make approximately 21 egg bites (a standard egg bit mold will hold 7 egg bites). Depending on the size of your air fryer, you may need to cook your egg bites in batches. Larger air fryers will hold more than one egg bite mold. The bites puff up while cooking and should slide right out of the silicone mold when finished.

PER SERVING: Calories: 149; Total fat: 11g; Saturated fat: 5g; Cholesterol: 219mg; Sodium: 383mg; Carbohydrates: 2g; Fiber: 0g; Protein: 11g

Glazed Ham Steaks

This simple, versatile recipe uses only five ingredients but has tons of flavor. You can serve it as a breakfast meat or a main course. It's great with eggs and toast for breakfast or with mashed potatoes and vegetables at dinner. You can also chop up any leftover ham and add it to the Sweet and Savory Breakfast Potatoes (page 21) for a filling brunch dish.

DAIRY-FREE, GLUTEN-FREE, 30 MINUTES OR LESS

PREP TIME: 5 minutes
COOK TIME: 15 minutes
SERVES 4
TEMPERATURE: 380°F

2 tablespoons maple syrup
½ tablespoon apple cider vinegar
½ tablespoon Dijon mustard
¼ tablespoon brown sugar
1 (1-pound) ham steak, fully cooked

1. Preheat the air fryer to 380°F.

2. In a small bowl, whisk together the maple syrup, vinegar, mustard, and brown sugar.

3. Remove the ham from the package and place it in the air fryer basket. Brush the marinade evenly over the top of the ham.

4. Air fry for 6 minutes. Flip the ham and brush with more marinade. Air fry for an additional 6 to 8 minutes, or until the ham is lightly browned and the glaze is caramelized.

Air Fryer Tip: Keep cleanup simple by washing the basket as soon as it cools so the sticky sugars don't harden up and become difficult to remove. If you are short on time, soak the basket in soapy water until you can wash it.

PER SERVING: Calories: 179; Total fat: 6g; Saturated fat: 2g; Cholesterol: 61mg; Sodium: 708mg; Carbohydrates: 9g; Fiber: <1g; Protein: 22g

Puffy Egg Tarts

Puff pastry is a light, flaky pastry you can find in the freezer section of your supermarket. It works well with both sweet and savory dishes. Using it instead of a homemade crust saves a lot of time and looks great. Thaw before use: Remove from the box and the outer wrapping and let it sit on the counter until the pastry unfolds easily but is still cold. This process should take less than 40 minutes.

VEGETARIAN

PREP TIME: 5 minutes
COOK TIME: 40 minutes
SERVES 4
TEMPERATURE: 380°F

2 tablespoons
   all-purpose flour
1 sheet frozen puff
   pastry, thawed
Extra-virgin olive oil, for
   the basket
1 cup shredded Monterey
   Jack cheese
4 large eggs
Salt
Freshly ground black pepper
1 tablespoon minced chives
   (optional)

1. Preheat the air fryer to 380°F.

2. Lightly flour your work surface. Unfold the thawed puff pastry sheet and cut it into 4 equal squares.

3. Lightly spray the air fryer basket with oil. Place 2 puff pastry squares in the basket.

4. Air fry for 8 to 10 minutes, or until golden brown.

5. Open the air fryer. Use a spoon to press down the center of the squares so there is a nice indentation. Sprinkle ¼ cup shredded cheese into the indentation in each square. Carefully crack an egg on top of the cheese. Season with salt and pepper.

6. Air fry for an additional 10 minutes, or until the eggs are cooked to your preference.

7. Top the egg tarts with chives, if using.

8. Repeat from step 3 with the remaining ingredients and serve.

Air Frying Tip: In step 6, air fry for 15 minutes for a hard yolk and firm egg whites, 12 minutes for a medium-cooked egg with a soft yolk and firm egg whites, and 10 minutes for an over-easy egg with a soft, runny yolk and barely firm egg whites.

PER SERVING: Calories: 437; Total fat: 29g; Saturated fat: 15g; Cholesterol: 212mg; Sodium: 442mg; Carbohydrates: 34g; Fiber: 2g; Protein: 18g

Cinnamon and Sugar Doughnuts

Save yourself a trip to the bakery and make these doughnuts from the comfort of your home. My family was in awe of how delicious these cinnamon and sugar treats turned out in the air fryer. They are a new favorite at our house. Bonus: you can also cook the donut holes to make another sweet treat!

VEGETARIAN, 30 MINUTES OR LESS

PREP TIME: 10 minutes
COOK TIME: 10 minutes
SERVES 4
TEMPERATURE: 350°F

1 tablespoon ground cinnamon
⅔ cup granulated sugar
1 (8-count) can large flaky biscuits
Extra-virgin olive oil, for the basket
5 tablespoons butter, melted

1. Preheat the air fryer to 350°F.

2. In a small bowl, combine the cinnamon and sugar and set aside.

3. Remove the biscuits from the can and place on a sheet of parchment paper. Use a 1-inch round biscuit cutter to cut a hole out of the center of each biscuit to make a doughnut. If you do not have a biscuit cutter, you can use a bottle cap.

4. Lightly spray the air fryer basket with oil. Place the doughnuts in a single layer in the basket, leaving ½ inch between each to ensure even cooking. (Do not discard the parchment paper.)

5. Air fry for 5 to 7 minutes, or until golden brown.

6. Transfer the doughnuts back to the parchment paper. Brush with the melted butter, making sure to coat all sides.

7. Dip each doughnut in the cinnamon-sugar mixture until well coated.

8. Serve the doughnuts warm and store any leftovers in a covered container at room temperature for up to 3 days. You can warm them in the microwave for 20 to 30 seconds.

PER SERVING: Calories: 600; Total fat: 26g; Saturated fat: 14g; Cholesterol: 38mg; Sodium: 1,035mg; Carbohydrates: 85g; Fiber: 1g; Protein: 6g

Crispy Prosciutto Egg Cups

Prosciutto is an Italian dry-cured ham that is packed with flavor. You can buy thinly sliced prosciutto packaged or have it freshly sliced at your supermarket's deli counter. Paired with eggs and with a boost of flavor and nutrients from the spinach, this dish is a well-rounded breakfast you can enjoy again and again. The prosciutto imparts a lot of salty flavor, so there is no need to add extra salt.

DAIRY-FREE, GLUTEN-FREE, 30 MINUTES OR LESS

PREP TIME: 10 minutes
COOK TIME: 15 minutes
SERVES 6
TEMPERATURE: 350°F

12 slices prosciutto
1½ cups fresh baby
    spinach leaves
12 medium eggs
Freshly ground black pepper

1. Preheat the air fryer to 350°F.

2. Press 1 slice of prosciutto into a silicone muffin cup so it creates a lining on the bottom and sides of the cup. Repeat with the remaining prosciutto.

3. Place 4 to 6 spinach leaves in the bottom of each cup.

4. Crack 1 egg into each cup. Season with pepper.

5. Gently place the muffin cups in the air fryer basket. Cook in batches, depending on how many muffin cups your basket will hold. Do not overcrowd.

6. Air fry for 10 to 15 minutes, or until the eggs are cooked to your preference.

Air Frying Tip: Transferring full silicone muffin cups to the air fryer basket can be challenging. Another option is to place the muffin cups in the basket before adding the egg to each cup. Once the muffin cups are in the air fryer, crack an egg into a small bowl and pour it into an egg muffin cup. Repeat with the remaining eggs.

PER SERVING: Calories: 171; Total fat: 11g; Saturated fat: 4g; Cholesterol: 339mg; Sodium: 391mg; Carbohydrates: 1g; Fiber: <1g; Protein: 15g

Ham and Swiss Quiche Cups

Ham and Swiss is a classic, delicious pairing. Add some eggs into the mix and you have a breakfast dish that is bursting with flavor and couldn't be easier. Serve these mini quiches to guests for brunch or make them ahead for on-the-go breakfasts during the week. As a bonus, all the ingredients are mixed in the same bowl, so cleanup is quick and easy.

GLUTEN-FREE, 30 MINUTES OR LESS

PREP TIME: 10 minutes
COOK TIME: 15 minutes
SERVES 6
TEMPERATURE: 330°F

Extra-virgin olive oil, for the muffin cups
6 large eggs, beaten
2 tablespoons milk
1 teaspoon minced garlic
½ teaspoon freshly ground black pepper
2 cups diced cooked ham
1 cup shredded Swiss cheese

1. Preheat the air fryer to 330°F. Lightly spray 12 silicone muffin cups with olive oil.

2. In a medium bowl, whisk together the eggs and milk. Stir in the garlic, pepper, ham, and cheese.

3. Fill each muffin cup with ¼ cup of the mixture until they are approximately three-quarters full.

4. Place the filled muffin cups in the air fryer basket, leaving a little room between each to ensure even cooking. (Air fry in batches, if necessary.)

5. Air fry for 10 to 12 minutes, or until the eggs are set and tops are golden brown.

Air Frying Tip: Silicone muffin cups work perfectly in the air fryer. They are sturdy enough to move around and they help make portion control a breeze.

PER SERVING: Calories: 203; Total fat: 13g; Saturated fat: 6g; Cholesterol: 206mg; Sodium: 570mg; Carbohydrates: 1g; Fiber: 0g; Protein: 21g

French Toast Sticks

French Toast Sticks are not just for children; adults will also be hooked on their delicious crunchiness. Serve with traditional pancake syrup for dipping or try drizzling honey over them. They also taste great with a dusting of confectioners' sugar and can be eaten for breakfast or even as a fun dessert!

VEGETARIAN, 30 MINUTES OR LESS

PREP TIME: 15 minutes
COOK TIME: 10 minutes
SERVES 4
TEMPERATURE: 400°F

4 slices firm bread
2 large eggs
¼ cup milk
1 tablespoon brown sugar
1 teaspoon ground cinnamon
¼ teaspoon salt
2 teaspoons vanilla extract
Extra-virgin olive oil, for the basket

1. Preheat the air fryer to 400°F.

2. Cut each bread slice into 3 thick sticks, then set aside.

3. In a medium shallow bowl, whisk together the eggs, milk, brown sugar, cinnamon, salt, and vanilla until they form a smooth batter.

4. Dip each bread stick into the egg batter, making sure to coat all sides.

5. Lightly spray the air fryer basket with oil. Place the coated bread sticks in a single layer in the basket, leaving ½ inch between each to ensure even cooking. (Air fry in batches, if necessary.)

6. Air fry for 4 minutes. Flip the sticks and air fry for an additional 2 to 4 minutes, or until golden brown and crispy.

Air Frying Tip: The cook time will vary based on the thickness of the bread. Check halfway through the cook time to avoid overcooking.

PER SERVING: Calories: 175; Total fat: 5g; Saturated fat: 1g; Cholesterol: 95mg; Sodium: 396mg; Carbohydrates: 25g; Fiber: 2g; Protein: 8g

Homemade Sausage Patties

You can turn ground pork into delicious homemade breakfast sausage patties in no time. Add a sausage patty to a toasted bagel or an English muffin for a quick breakfast sandwich when you're on the go, or make up a big breakfast platter with sausage patties, scrambled eggs, and biscuits.

DAIRY-FREE, GLUTEN-FREE

PREP TIME: 15 minutes
COOK TIME: 20 minutes
SERVES 4
TEMPERATURE: 400°F

1 pound ground pork
1 teaspoon salt
1 teaspoon freshly ground
   black pepper
¾ teaspoon garlic powder
½ teaspoon ground sage
¼ teaspoon ground thyme
¼ teaspoon ground red
   pepper flakes

1. Preheat the air fryer to 400°F.

2. In a large bowl, combine the pork, salt, black pepper, garlic powder, sage, thyme, and red pepper flakes. Using your hands, mix the seasonings evenly into the pork. Avoid overworking the meat.

3. Divide the seasoned pork into ¼-cup portions, roll each portion into a ball, and press it down slightly to form a patty.

4. Place the patties in a single layer in the air fryer basket, leaving a little space between each to ensure even cooking.

5. Air fry for 10 minutes. Flip the patties and air fry for an additional 5 to 8 minutes, or until the pork reaches an internal temperature of 160°F.

Air Frying Tip: For the best results, use an instant-read meat thermometer. If the patties are releasing a lot of grease, you can add a few tablespoons of water to the bottom of the air fryer basket to reduce any smoking.

Variation: If you like a sweet breakfast sausage patty, mix 2 to 3 teaspoons of maple syrup into the meat mixture in step 2.

PER SERVING: Calories: 250; Total fat: 18g; Saturated fat: 6g; Cholesterol: 77mg; Sodium: 667mg; Carbohydrates: 1g; Fiber: <1g; Protein: 21g

Seasoned Radish Hash Browns

The strong bite of raw radishes is significantly mellowed when they are cooked. When they are cooked hash brown-style, the results are very similar to traditional potato hash browns. If you are watching your carbohydrates, this alternative offers you the great taste without all the starch.

DAIRY-FREE, GLUTEN-FREE, VEGAN

PREP TIME: 20 minutes
COOK TIME: 20 minutes
SERVES 4
TEMPERATURE: 400°F

2 pounds radishes
2 tablespoons extra-virgin olive oil, plus more for the basket
1½ teaspoons garlic powder
1½ teaspoons onion powder
1½ teaspoons paprika
1 teaspoon salt
1 teaspoon freshly ground black pepper

1. Preheat the air fryer to 400°F.

2. Cut the roots and stems off the radishes. Use a mandoline or food processor to cut the radishes into thin slices.

3. In a large bowl, combine the radish slices with the olive oil, garlic powder, onion powder, paprika, salt, and pepper. Stir to evenly coat the radishes in the oil and seasonings.

4. Lightly spray the air fryer basket with oil. Place half the seasoned radish slices in the basket. (To ensure even cooking, cook the hash browns in two batches.)

5. Air fry for 5 minutes. Shake the basket to redistribute the hash browns. Lightly spray with oil and air fry for an additional 5 minutes.

6. Repeat steps 4 and 5 with the remaining batch.

Air Frying Tip: The radish slices become tender and delicious after about 10 minutes in the air fryer. If you like your vegetables roasted and slightly charred, add about 5 minutes to the cook time.

PER SERVING: Calories: 107; Total fat: 7g; Saturated fat: 1g; Cholesterol: 0mg; Sodium: 680mg; Carbohydrates: 10g; Fiber: 4g; Protein: 2g

Stuffed Breakfast Bell Peppers

A stuffed bell pepper is a full meal in an edible bowl. My version uses breakfast ingredients for a fun twist on the classic, wonderful for a savory brunch served with a simple green salad or Sweet and Savory Breakfast Potatoes (page 21).

GLUTEN-FREE, 30 MINUTES OR LESS

PREP TIME: 15 minutes
COOK TIME: 15 minutes
SERVES 4
TEMPERATURE: 350°F

2 red bell peppers
Salt
Freshly ground black pepper
4 tablespoons crumbled cooked bacon
8 tablespoons shredded mozzarella cheese
4 large eggs
Extra-virgin olive oil, for the basket
4 teaspoons finely chopped fresh chives, for garnish (optional)

1. Preheat the air fryer to 350°F.

2. Cut the bell peppers in half lengthwise from stem to base. Pop out the stem, then remove the seeds and membranes so each half looks like a shallow bowl.

3. Season the inside of each bell pepper half with salt and black pepper to taste.

4. Sprinkle 1 tablespoon chopped bacon into each bell pepper half, followed by 2 tablespoons mozzarella cheese.

5. Carefully crack one egg into each bell pepper half.

6. Lightly spray the air fryer basket with oil. Place the bell pepper halves in a single layer in the basket.

7. Air fry for 10 to 15 minutes, or until the eggs are cooked to your preference.

8. Sprinkle each stuffed pepper with 1 teaspoon chives, if using, and serve.

Air Frying Tip: Every air fryer will cook differently, so it is important to watch your eggs closely to achieve the level of doneness you desire.

PER SERVING: Calories: 161; Total fat: 11g; Saturated fat: 5g; Cholesterol: 204mg; Sodium: 249mg; Carbohydrates: 5g; Fiber: 1g; Protein: 12g

Easy Veggie Omelet

You don't have to make omelets on the stove. Grab a small oven-safe baking pan that fits in your air fryer and you're on your way. Using the air fryer makes cleanup a breeze, too. Pair this veggie omelet with Homemade Sausage Patties (page 32) and Savory Cheddar-Bacon Muffins (page 226) for a complete meal.

GLUTEN-FREE, VEGETARIAN,
30 MINUTES OR LESS

PREP TIME: 10 minutes
COOK TIME: 10 minutes
SERVES 1
TEMPERATURE: 350°F

2 large eggs
¼ cup milk
½ cup shredded
   cheddar cheese
2 tablespoons diced
   mushrooms
2 tablespoons diced red
   bell pepper
1 tablespoon diced
   scallions, white and pale
   green parts, plus deep
   green parts for garnish
Salt
Freshly ground black pepper
Extra-virgin olive oil,
   for the pan

1. Preheat the air fryer to 350°F.

2. In a medium bowl, whisk together the eggs and milk. Add the cheese, mushrooms, bell pepper, and diced scallions and stir. Add salt and black pepper to taste.

3. Generously spray a 6-inch-by-3-inch baking pan with oil. Pour the egg mixture into the pan.

4. Place the baking pan in the air fryer basket.

5. Air fry for 6 minutes, then start checking the omelet every minute until the eggs are set. When it is fully cooked, usually 6 to 8 minutes, a toothpick inserted in the middle should come out clean.

6. Carefully slide the omelet onto a plate. Serve flat, garnished with sliced scallions, if using.

Variation: You can add any omelet filling you desire to this recipe. Try crumbled cooked bacon, sausage, or ham if you want to try it with meat.

PER SERVING: Calories: 427; Total fat: 32g; Saturated fat: 15g; Cholesterol: 435mg; Sodium: 521mg; Carbohydrates: 7g; Fiber: 1g; Protein: 28g

Sun-Dried Tomato Frittata

The sweet, tangy flavor of sun-dried tomatoes combines perfectly with fresh basil and mozzarella cheese to make a delectable breakfast frittata. Serve with Seasoned Radish Hash Browns (page 33) or a simple green salad.

GLUTEN-FREE, VEGETARIAN, 30 MINUTES OR LESS

PREP TIME: 10 minutes
COOK TIME: 10 minutes
SERVES 2
TEMPERATURE: 350°F

Extra-virgin olive oil, for the pan
4 large eggs
3 tablespoons heavy (whipping) cream
2 tablespoons chopped fresh basil
¾ cup shredded mozzarella cheese
⅓ cup oil-packed sun-dried tomatoes, patted dry and chopped fine
Salt
Freshly ground black pepper

1. Preheat the air fryer to 350°F. Generously spray a 6-inch-by-3-inch round baking pan with oil.

2. In a medium bowl, whisk together the eggs and cream. Add the basil, cheese, sun-dried tomatoes, salt, and pepper and stir to combine.

3. Pour the egg mixture into the prepared pan. Place the pan in the air fryer basket.

4. Air fry for 10 to 12 minutes, or until the top is golden and a toothpick inserted in the middle comes out clean.

Air Frying Tip: You can use any oven-safe baking pan that will fit in your air fryer basket. If you prefer to make individual frittatas, use a smaller pan, reduce the cook time by 1 to 2 minutes and air fry in batches.

PER SERVING: Calories: 405; Total fat: 32g; Saturated fat: 15g; Cholesterol: 436mg; Sodium: 479mg; Carbohydrates: 7g; Fiber: 1g; Protein: 23g

Scotch Eggs

Scotch eggs are a traditional deep-fried British dish commonly taken on picnics and served in pubs. Making Scotch eggs in the air fryer reduces the amount of oil used, but still results in a crispy meat-wrapped egg. They make a wonderful savory breakfast treat or snack.

30 MINUTES OR LESS

PREP TIME: 20 minutes
COOK TIME: 10 minutes
SERVES 4
TEMPERATURE: 400°F

1 pound bulk pork sausage
1 tablespoon finely
   chopped chives
1 teaspoon dried
   minced onion
½ teaspoon salt
½ teaspoon freshly ground
   black pepper
¼ cup all-purpose flour
1 large egg
¾ cup panko bread crumbs
4 hard-boiled eggs
Extra-virgin olive oil, for
   spraying

1. Preheat the air fryer to 400°F.

2. In a medium bowl, combine the sausage, chives, onion, salt, and pepper. Gently mix until well combined. Shape the mixture into 4 equal-size patties.

3. Put the flour into a small shallow bowl.

4. In a second small shallow bowl, beat the egg.

5. Put the bread crumbs in a third small shallow bowl.

6. Pat dry the hard-boiled eggs with a paper towel. Roll each egg in the flour to coat.

7. Place one flour-coated egg on each sausage patty. Wrap the sausage patty around the egg so it completely encases the egg.

8. Coat the sausage-encased egg in the beaten egg, then in the bread crumbs.

9. Lightly spray the air fryer basket with oil. Place the Scotch eggs in a single layer in the basket. Lightly spray with oil.

10. Air fry for 6 minutes. Flip the Scotch eggs and lightly spray with oil. Air fry for an additional 5 to 6 minutes, or until the sausage is fully cooked.

PER SERVING: Calories: 433; Total fat: 27g; Saturated fat: 8g; Cholesterol: 294mg; Sodium: 964mg; Carbohydrates: 18g; Fiber: 1g; Protein: 26g

Ham and Cheddar Breakfast Pockets

Crescent dough is a quick and delicious way to make a grab-and-go breakfast pocket. I like using ham and cheese as a classic and tasty filling. This recipe is a great way to use up leftover Glazed Ham Steaks (page 23), or feel free to try it with other cheeses and cooked breakfast meats.

30 MINUTES OR LESS

PREP TIME: 10 minutes
COOK TIME: 10 minutes
SERVES 4
TEMPERATURE: 350°F

2 (8-ounce) cans crescent rolls, refrigerated
8 tablespoons shredded cheddar cheese, divided
4 tablespoons diced cooked ham, divided
Extra-virgin olive oil, for spraying

1. Preheat the air fryer to 350°F.

2. Open the crescent roll tubes and unroll each crescent triangle. You should have 16 triangles.

3. Place 1 tablespoon cheese and ½ tablespoon ham in the center of 8 crescent triangles.

4. Place the remaining 8 crescent triangles on top each filled triangle and press all the edges together to seal the toppings inside the pocket.

5. Lightly spray the air fryer basket with oil. Place the breakfast pockets in a single layer in the basket. Do not overcrowd. (Air fry in batches, if necessary.) Lightly spray with oil.

6. Air fry for 5 minutes. Flip the pockets and lightly spray with oil. Air fry for an additional 3 to 5 minutes, or until the crescent dough is fully cooked and the tops are golden brown.

PER SERVING: Calories: 472; Total fat: 26g; Saturated fat: 11g; Cholesterol: 20mg; Sodium: 1,052mg; Carbohydrates: 49g; Fiber: 0g; Protein: 14g

Lunch and Light Fare

Stromboli

Stromboli is an Italian-American savory turnover stuffed with cheese, sauce, and a variety of other fillings. When made in the air fryer, it is a fast and filling meal. In this version, thin-crust pizza dough is wrapped around savory pizza sauce, creamy mozzarella, spicy pepperoni, and earthy mushrooms.

PREP TIME: 10 minutes
COOK TIME: 25 minutes
SERVES 4
TEMPERATURE: 360°F

1 (11-ounce) tube thin-crust
  pizza dough, refrigerated
¼ cup pizza sauce
¼ cup diced mushrooms
¼ cup mini pepperoni
1 cup shredded
  mozzarella cheese
1 egg yolk
1 tablespoon milk
Extra-virgin olive oil, for
  the basket

1. Preheat the air fryer to 360°F.

2. Unroll the pizza dough on a flat surface. Cut the dough in half lengthwise so you have two rectangles.

3. Leaving a ½-inch border around the edges, spread half the pizza sauce over one half of one piece of the dough. Repeat on the other piece of dough.

4. Sprinkle half the mushrooms, pepperoni, and mozzarella over the sauce on each piece of dough.

5. Fold the untopped side of the dough over so it covers the toppings. Seal the edges with your fingers or a fork so the sauce, mushrooms, pepperoni, and cheese are securely encased in the dough.

6. In a small bowl, whisk the egg yolk and milk until well combined.

7. Brush the egg wash on top of each stromboli.

8. Lightly spray the air fryer basket with oil. Place one stromboli in the basket.

9. Air fry for 5 minutes. Flip the stromboli and brush with egg wash. Air fry for an additional 5 to 7 minutes, or until golden brown.

10. Repeat steps 8 and 9 with the remaining stromboli.

Air Frying Tip: Very few air fryers are large enough to hold one long stromboli. It is important to cut the pizza dough into two pieces and make two smaller stromboli that will fit in the air fryer basket.

Variation: This recipe is so easy to customize. Add any chopped vegetables and cooked meats you like. Try to stick with about ½ cup of total fillings in addition to the cheese.

PER SERVING: Calories: 358; Total fat: 15g; Saturated fat: 7g; Cholesterol: 74mg; Sodium: 747mg; Carbohydrates: 40g; Fiber: <1g; Protein: 15g

Hot Ham and Cheese Sandwiches

Nothing tastes better on a cold day than a hot ham and cheese sandwich with a bowl of soup. If you love a crispy hot sandwich for lunch, grab some sourdough bread and head over to your air fryer. This version is crunchy, delicious, and oh-so-easy to make.

PREP TIME: 5 minutes
COOK TIME: 30 minutes
SERVES 4
TEMPERATURE: 350°F

8 tablespoons unsalted butter, room temperature
8 slices sourdough bread
16 slices Colby-Jack cheese
8 slices ham

1. Preheat the air fryer to 350°F.

2. Butter one side of each slice of bread.

3. Place 2 slices of bread buttered side down in the air fryer basket. Place a slice of cheese on top of each slice of bread, then layer a slice of meat and top with another slice of cheese. Top with another slice of bread, buttered side up.

4. Air fry for 6 to 7 minutes. Flip the sandwiches and air fry for an additional 6 to 7 minutes, or until the bread is crispy and golden brown.

5. Repeat steps 2 through 4 with the remaining sandwiches.

Variation: Feel free to replace the sliced ham with any sliced cooked meat. Swap out the Colby-Jack cheese with another variety. If you want a very hearty sandwich, double the meat!

PER SERVING: Calories: 767; Total fat: 53g; Saturated fat: 32g; Cholesterol: 163mg; Sodium: 1,806mg; Carbohydrates: 37g; Fiber: 1g; Protein: 36g

Cheese and Black Bean Quesadillas

Quesadillas are a beloved light meal for kids and adults alike. This meat-free version with black beans and cheese is a quick handheld lunch that will help get you through the afternoon. It's also a great healthy after-school snack option, especially if your kids have activities. The salsa verde gives this quesadilla a wonderful little kick, but feel free to use any salsa of your choosing.

VEGETARIAN, 30 MINUTES OR LESS

PREP TIME: 10 minutes
COOK TIME: 20 minutes
SERVES 2
TEMPERATURE: 350°F

1 (15-ounce) can black beans, drained and rinsed
½ cup canned corn, drained
½ cup salsa verde, plus more for serving
¼ teaspoon cumin
4 (8-inch) flour tortillas
Extra-virgin olive oil, for spraying
1 cup shredded Monterey Jack cheese, divided
Sour cream, for serving

1. Preheat the air fryer to 350°F.

2. In a medium bowl, mash half the beans roughly with a fork. Mix in the remaining beans, corn, salsa verde, and cumin.

3. Spread ½ cup of the bean filling evenly over 2 tortillas.

4. Lightly spray the air fryer basket with oil. Carefully place one of the tortillas with the bean filling in the basket. Sprinkle ½ cup shredded cheese over the beans. Place another plain tortilla on top and press down so it seals to the cheese and bean mixture. Lightly spray with oil.

5. Air fry for 5 minutes. Flip the quesadilla and lightly spray with oil. Air fry for an additional 3 to 5 minutes, or until both sides are lightly browned and crispy and the cheese has melted.

6. Repeat steps 4 and 5 with the remaining ingredients. Serve with sour cream and additional salsa.

Air Frying Tip: Lightweight ingredients like tortillas may move around in the air fryer because of the air circulation. After a minute of cooking, check to make sure the top tortilla is not shifting. Once the cheese starts melting, it won't be an issue.

PER SERVING: Calories: 769; Total fat: 27g; Saturated fat: 14g; Cholesterol: 50mg; Sodium: 1,688mg; Carbohydrates: 98g; Fiber: 21g; Protein: 36g

Sausage Rolls

Sausage Rolls are a two-ingredient recipe that couldn't be easier to make. This classic snack always reminds me of childhood and quick summer lunches before heading out to the pool. For a heartier meal, these rolls pair perfectly with Onion Rings (page 79).

DAIRY-FREE, 30 MINUTES OR LESS

PREP TIME: 10 minutes
COOK TIME: 10 minutes
SERVES 4
TEMPERATURE: 350°F

1 (8-ounce) container crescent rolls, refrigerated
1 (8-count) package beef hot dogs
Extra-virgin olive oil, for the basket

1. Preheat the air fryer to 350°F.

2. Open the container of crescent rolls and separate the dough into triangles. Wrap one dough triangle around each hot dog.

3. Lightly spray the air fryer basket with oil. Place the wrapped hot dogs in a single layer in the basket, leaving ¼ inch between each to ensure even cooking.

4. Air fry for 5 minutes. Flip the sausage rolls and air fry for an additional 3 to 5 minutes, or until the dough is cooked through and golden brown.

Variation: It is easy to turn these sausage rolls into a vegan lunch by replacing the hot dogs with plant-based hot dogs. The crescent dough does not contain dairy and is considered vegan.

PER SERVING: Calories: 484; Total fat: 35g; Saturated fat: 14g; Cholesterol: 52mg; Sodium: 1,219mg; Carbohydrates: 27g; Fiber: 0g; Protein: 13g

Chicken Fritter Sliders

Miniature chicken burgers are such fun. My family loves these juicy, flavorful chicken fritters served on slider buns. With two cheeses and Cajun seasoning, you get flavor packed into every bite. Serve with all your favorite burger condiments and a simple green salad, Creole Carrot Fries (page 176), or Roasted Beet Chips (page 185).

30 MINUTES OR LESS

PREP TIME: 10 minutes
COOK TIME: 15 minutes
SERVES 3
TEMPERATURE: 350°F

1 pound ground chicken
½ cup panko bread crumbs
¼ cup shredded
    Parmesan cheese
¼ cup shredded
    mozzarella cheese
1 teaspoon Cajun seasoning
½ teaspoon dill weed
Extra-virgin olive oil, for
    the basket
1 package slider buns

1. Preheat the air fryer to 350°F.

2. In a large bowl, combine the chicken, panko bread crumbs, Parmesan, mozzarella, Cajun seasoning, and dill weed.

3. Divide the seasoned chicken into ¼-cup portions. Roll each portion into a ball and press it down slightly to form a patty. You should have 6 or 7 patties.

4. Lightly spray the air fryer basket with oil. Place the sliders in a single layer in the basket.

5. Air fry for 7 minutes. Flip the sliders and air fry for an additional 5 to 8 minutes, or until golden brown.

6. Serve on slider buns with your choice of condiments.

Variation: If you want to bring some additional heat to these sliders, add ⅛ to ¼ teaspoon of cayenne pepper to the meat mixture in step 2.

PER SERVING: Calories: 765; Total fat: 27g; Saturated fat: 7g; Cholesterol: 152mg; Sodium: 996mg; Carbohydrates: 92g; Fiber: 4g; Protein: 52g

Warm Caprese Toast

Caprese is a delicious Italian salad make with fresh tomatoes, basil, and mozzarella. It's usually dressed simply with extra-virgin olive oil and sometimes a splash of balsamic vinegar. My take on this classic dish is served warm on toasted bread with delicious melted mozzarella cheese. It's a fast and easy lunch that is also pretty enough to serve to guests.

VEGETARIAN, 30 MINUTES OR LESS

PREP TIME: 10 minutes
COOK TIME: 10 minutes
SERVES 4
TEMPERATURE: 350°F

2 tablespoons extra-virgin olive oil, plus more for spraying

2 tablespoons balsamic vinegar

2 teaspoons minced garlic

3 Roma tomatoes, thinly sliced

1 loaf crusty Italian bread, cut into 12 slices

12 slices fresh mozzarella cheese

1 cup fresh basil leaves, or fresh baby spinach leaves

1. Preheat the air fryer to 350°F.

2. In a small shallow bowl, combine the extra-virgin olive oil with the balsamic vinegar and garlic. Add the sliced tomatoes to the bowl and set aside.

3. Lightly spray the air fryer basket with oil. Place the bread slices in a single layer in the basket. Lightly spray with oil.

4. Air fry for 4 to 6 minutes, or until the bread is lightly browned and toasted. Place one slice of cheese on top of each piece of toasted bread.

5. Air fry for an additional 3 to 4 minutes, or until the cheese has softened and started to melt.

6. Top with the basil and marinated tomato slices and serve.

PER SERVING: Calories: 522; Total fat: 26g; Saturated fat: 11g; Cholesterol: 56mg; Sodium: 947mg; Carbohydrates: 50g; Fiber: 4g; Protein: 22g

Pork Tenderloin Lettuce Wraps

Pork tenderloin is a moist and tender meat that absorbs the flavors of a marinade beautifully. This marinade combines the salty sweetness of hoisin with the heat of sriracha and the piquancy of ginger. The lettuce provides a mild and cooling complement to the marinated pork and is a simple low-carb alternative to the standard bun.

DAIRY-FREE

PREP TIME: 20 minutes

COOK TIME: 20 minutes, plus up to 2 hours to marinate

SERVES 4

TEMPERATURE: 360°F

1 pound pork tenderloin, trimmed of visible fat

¼ cup hoisin sauce

2 teaspoons sriracha

½ teaspoon minced fresh ginger

Extra-virgin olive oil, for the basket

1 head butter lettuce

1. Slice the pork tenderloin into strips, 2 inches long and ½ inch thick.

2. In a large bowl, combine the hoisin sauce, sriracha, and ginger. Add the pork and mix to coat. Refrigerate for at least 30 minutes or up to 2 hours.

3. Preheat the air fryer to 360°F.

4. Lightly spray the air fryer basket with oil. Place the marinated pork in a single layer in the basket.

5. Air fry for 15 to 20 minutes, stirring every 5 minutes, until the pork is cooked through and reaches an internal temperature of 145°F.

6. Place approximately ¼ cup of cooked pork strips on a large lettuce leaf, roll it up, and serve.

Variation: The pork tenderloin strips also taste great in a wrap. Simply put a leaf of lettuce and the pork in a tortilla-style wrap along with any other vegetables you enjoy, such as shredded carrots, sliced radishes, sliced cucumbers, or sliced sweet bell peppers, then roll it up for an on-the-go lunch.

PER SERVING: Calories: 168; Total fat: 3g; Saturated fat: 1g; Cholesterol: 74mg; Sodium: 388mg; Carbohydrates: 8g; Fiber: 1g; Protein: 25g

Crispy Fish Sandwiches

It is nice to have a classic crispy fish sandwich recipe on hand to make at home when the craving strikes. This sandwich is enough on its own for lunch or a light dinner. For a heartier meal, serve it with a quick coleslaw or a simple green salad.

30 MINUTES OR LESS

PREP TIME: 10 minutes
COOK TIME: 20 minutes
SERVES 4
TEMPERATURE: 400°F

4 (4-ounce) pollock or
   cod fillets
½ teaspoon salt, plus more
   for seasoning
½ teaspoon freshly ground
   black pepper, plus more
   for seasoning
½ cup all-purpose flour
2 large eggs
1 teaspoon water
1½ cups panko
   bread crumbs
1 teaspoon Old Bay
   seasoning
Extra-virgin olive oil, for
   spraying
4 hamburger buns
4 tablespoons tartar sauce
   (optional)

1. Preheat the air fryer to 400°F.

2. Season the fillets with a pinch each of salt and pepper.

3. In a small shallow bowl, mix together the flour salt, and pepper.

4. In a second small shallow bowl, whisk together the eggs and water with a pinch each of salt and pepper.

5. In a third small shallow bowl, combine the bread crumbs and Old Bay.

6. Coat each fillet in the seasoned flour, then in the egg, then in the bread crumbs.

7. Lightly spray the air fryer basket with oil. Place the fillets in a single layer in the basket. Lightly spray with oil.

8. Air fry for 8 to 10 minutes. Flip the fillets and lightly spray with oil. Air fry for an additional 5 to 10 minutes, until the breading is golden brown and crispy and the fish is cooked through.

9. Serve on a bun with the tartar sauce, if using.

Air Frying Tip: Fish is notorious for sticking to a pan, so do not forget to spray the air fryer basket with olive oil. If the fish still sticks to the basket, try using parchment paper liners.

PER SERVING: Calories: 422; Total fat: 5g; Saturated fat: 1g; Cholesterol: 163mg; Sodium: 840mg; Carbohydrates: 56g; Fiber: 2g; Protein: 34g

Chile-Lime Shrimp Soft Tacos

These shrimp tacos are bursting with bright, zesty flavors. Before you know it, this quick and easy dish will be a part of your regular repertoire. You can make the marinade ahead of time and keep it in the refrigerator until you are ready to add the shrimp, but never marinate the shrimp for longer than 30 minutes or they can become mushy.

30 MINUTES OR LESS

PREP TIME: 10 minutes
COOK TIME: 15 minutes
SERVES 4
TEMPERATURE: 400°F

2 tablespoons extra-virgin olive oil, plus more for the basket

3 tablespoons freshly squeezed lime juice

1 tablespoon honey

2 teaspoons minced garlic

1 teaspoon chili powder

½ teaspoon smoked paprika

¼ teaspoon salt

¼ teaspoon black pepper

1 pound medium cooked shrimp

8 (8-inch) flour tortillas

Sour cream, chopped lettuce, tomatoes, or cilantro, for topping (optional)

1. Preheat the air fryer to 400°F.

2. In a medium bowl, mix together the olive oil, lime juice, honey, garlic, chili powder, smoked paprika, salt, and pepper.

3. Add the shrimp and toss to coat.

4. Lightly spray the air fryer basket with oil. Place the shrimp in the basket.

5. Air fry for 5 minutes. Shake the basket and air fry for an additional 5 to 10 minutes, or until the shrimp are cooked through and starting to brown.

6. Warm the tortillas on the stove or in the microwave to your desired temperature.

7. Assemble the soft tacos by wrapping the shrimp and desired toppings in the warmed tortillas.

Variation: This recipe also makes a great salad. Simply skip the tortilla and toppings and arrange the shrimp on a bed of greens.

PER SERVING: Calories: 491; Total fat: 15g; Saturated fat: 4g; Cholesterol: 214mg; Sodium: 1,232mg; Carbohydrates: 55g; Fiber: 4g; Protein: 34g

Everything-but-the-Bagel Chicken Strips

Everything bagel seasoning typically combines sesame seeds, poppy seeds, dried onion, garlic, and salt to create a memorable savory flavor. In this recipe, the mixture coats classic chicken strips for an unforgettable snack. Serve with your favorite dipping sauce or try them on top of a green salad.

DAIRY-FREE

PREP TIME: 15 minutes
COOK TIME: 20 minutes
SERVES 4
TEMPERATURE: 370°F

1 large egg
1 cup panko bread crumbs
2 tablespoons everything bagel seasoning
1 pound chicken tenderloins
Extra-virgin olive oil, for spraying

1. Preheat the air fryer to 370°F.

2. In a small shallow bowl, whisk the egg.

3. In a second small shallow bowl, combine the bread crumbs and the everything bagel seasoning.

4. Coat the chicken in the egg, then in the bread crumb mixture.

5. Lightly spray the air fryer basket with oil. Place the breaded chicken in a single layer in the basket. Lightly spray with oil.

6. Air fry for 7 minutes. Flip the chicken and lightly spray with oil. Air fry for an additional 7 to 10 minutes, or until the breading is lightly browned and crispy and the chicken reaches an internal temperature of 165°F.

Air Frying Tip: Use silicone-tipped tongs to flip the chicken quickly and easily during cooking.

PER SERVING: Calories: 228; Total fat: 2g; Saturated fat: <1g; Cholesterol: 96mg; Sodium: 566mg; Carbohydrates: 15g; Fiber: 1g; Protein: 29g

Beef Fajita Salad

This salad is perfect for a light yet filling lunch. If you have leftover steak and veggies, eat them the next day in soft tacos or burritos.

DAIRY-FREE, GLUTEN-FREE

PREP TIME: 10 minutes
COOK TIME: 15 minutes, plus up to 2 hours to marinate
SERVES 4
TEMPERATURE: 390°F

For the beef and vegetables

¼ cup extra-virgin olive oil
¼ cup freshly squeezed orange juice
1 tablespoon chipotle seasoning
½ teaspoon cumin
1 tablespoon Worcestershire sauce
2 teaspoons minced garlic
½ tablespoon brown sugar
½ teaspoon liquid smoke
1 pound skirt steak, thinly sliced across the grain
2 bell peppers, sliced into strips
1 small onion, sliced into strips

To make the beef and vegetables

1. In a large bowl, combine the olive oil, orange juice, chipotle seasoning, cumin, Worcestershire sauce, garlic, brown sugar, and liquid smoke.

2. Add the sliced steak, bell peppers, and onion. Coat with the marinade, cover the bowl, and refrigerate for at least 30 minutes or up to 2 hours.

3. Remove the crisper plate from the air fryer basket. Preheat the air fryer to 390°F.

4. Lightly spray the air fryer basket with oil. Place the marinated steak and vegetables directly in the basket.

5. Air fry for 5 minutes. Shake the basket to redistribute the meat. Air fry for an additional 5 to 10 minutes, or until the steak is cooked to your preference.

CONTINUED

For the salad

4 cups chopped
    romaine lettuce

1 avocado, pitted, peeled,
    and thinly sliced

1 large tomato, diced

Dressing of your choice

To make the salads

6. Divide the romaine lettuce equally among four
   bowls. Top each serving with an equal portion
   of the sliced avocado, tomato, steak, peppers,
   onions, and dressing.

Air Frying Tip: Removing the crisper plate lets the meat and
vegetables cook in the juices of the marinade, which makes
them juicy and flavorful. If you prefer the meat a bit drier,
leave the crisper plate in.

PER SERVING: Calories: 428; Total fat: 30g; Saturated fat: 7g;
Cholesterol: 75mg; Sodium: 251mg; Carbohydrates: 16g; Fiber: 5g;
Protein: 26g

Breaded Spicy Chicken Sandwiches

Skip the drive-through window! Instead, make your own crispy, spicy breaded chicken sandwiches in minutes with your air fryer. The spice in this sandwich is just right, but you can always kick it up a level by adding some extra cayenne pepper. Serve with your favorite toppings, like lettuce, tomato, and pickle.

PREP TIME: 20 minutes
COOK TIME: 15 minutes
SERVES 4
TEMPERATURE: 390°F

2 boneless, skinless
   chicken breasts
2 teaspoons salt, plus more
   for seasoning
1 teaspoon freshly ground
   black pepper, plus more
   for seasoning
2 large eggs
1 tablespoon milk
1 teaspoon hot sauce
1 cup all-purpose flour
1 teaspoon paprika
1 teaspoon cayenne pepper
Extra-virgin olive oil, for
   spraying
4 large buns

1. Preheat the air fryer to 390°F.

2. Cut the chicken breasts in half so you have 4 thinner breasts. Using a meat mallet, pound each piece to an even size and thickness. Season with salt and black pepper to taste.

3. In a small shallow bowl, whisk together the eggs, milk, and hot sauce.

4. In another small shallow bowl, combine the flour, salt, black pepper, paprika, and cayenne pepper.

5. Coat each chicken breast in the egg mixture, then in the flour mixture. Repeat this process until each chicken breast is double coated.

6. Lightly spray the air fryer basket with oil. Arrange the breaded chicken breasts in a single layer in the basket. Liberally spray with oil.

7. Air fry for 6 minutes. Flip the chicken and spray with oil. Air fry for an additional 6 to 8 minutes, or until the breading is golden brown and crispy and the chicken reaches an internal temperature of 165°F.

8. Place the chicken breasts on the buns and serve.

Variation: You can reduce the spice by leaving out the hot sauce and cayenne pepper.

PER SERVING: Calories: 419; Total fat: 8g; Saturated fat: 2g; Cholesterol: 133mg; Sodium: 1,572mg; Carbohydrates: 54g; Fiber: 3g; Protein: 31g

Falafel Bites

Falafel is a Middle Eastern food made from chickpeas (and sometimes fava beans), herbs, and spices. It is deep-fried and served on pita bread, often with chopped cucumber, tomatoes, and hummus. This version creates a crispy patty without all the added fat from deep frying.

VEGETARIAN

PREP TIME: 30 minutes, plus up to 3 hours to chill
COOK TIME: 10 minutes
SERVES 4
TEMPERATURE: 350°F

1 (15-ounce) can chickpeas, drained and rinsed
1 tablespoon minced garlic
1 small onion, coarsely chopped
¼ cup fresh parsley, roughly chopped
¼ cup fresh cilantro, roughly chopped
1 teaspoon ground cumin
¼ teaspoon cayenne pepper
½ teaspoon salt
¼ teaspoon freshly ground black pepper
1 teaspoon baking powder
2 to 4 tablespoons bread crumbs
Extra-virgin olive oil, for spraying

1. Put the chickpeas on a paper towel and pat dry.

2. Place the chickpeas, garlic, onion, parsley, cilantro, cumin, cayenne pepper, salt, and black pepper in the bowl of a food processor and process until a thick, chunky paste forms.

3. Transfer the falafel mixture to a medium bowl and stir in the baking powder. Stir in 2 tablespoons bread crumbs. If the mixture won't hold its shape enough to come together in patties, add the remaining 2 tablespoons bread crumbs.

4. Cover the bowl and refrigerate for at least 1 hour.

5. Preheat the air fryer to 350°F.

6. Scoop out approximately 2 tablespoons of the mixture and form it into a ball. Repeat until you've used all the mixture. You should have about 12 equal-size balls. Flatten the balls slightly to form patties.

7. Lightly spray the air fryer basket with oil. Place the falafel bites in a single layer in the basket, leaving about ¼ inch between each to ensure even cooking.

8. Lightly spray with oil and air fry for 6 minutes. Flip the falafel and lightly spray with oil. Air fry for an additional 6 minutes, or until golden brown.

PER SERVING: Calories: 121; Total fat: 2g; Saturated fat: <1g; Cholesterol: 0mg; Sodium: 586mg; Carbohydrates: 20g; Fiber: 5g; Protein: 6g

Bagel Pizzas

Bagel pizzas are the perfect lunch for busy days. Kids and adults alike will gobble them up. You can use any of your favorite pizza toppings, so get creative or set up a pizza bar and let your family or guests pick their own.

VEGETARIAN, 30 MINUTES OR LESS

PREP TIME: 5 minutes
COOK TIME: 5 minutes
SERVES 3
TEMPERATURE: 350°F

3 bagels
1½ cups pizza sauce
1½ cups mozzarella cheese
Extra-virgin olive oil, for the basket
Mushrooms, sliced olives, diced ham, mini pepperoni, bell peppers, or onions, for topping (optional)

1. Preheat the air fryer to 350°F.

2. Split each bagel in half. Spread 2 to 3 tablespoons pizza sauce over each bagel half.

3. Lightly spray the air fryer basket with oil. Place the bagel halves in a single layer in the basket. (Air fry in batches, if necessary.) Sprinkle ¼ cup cheese and your desired toppings on top of each bagel.

4. Air fry for 5 minutes, or until the cheese has melted.

Variation: Switch up the flavor of your pizzas by using cheese bagels, garlic bagels, onion bagels, or everything bagels.

....

PER SERVING: Calories: 525; Total fat: 17g; Saturated fat: 10g; Cholesterol: 50mg; Sodium: 1,283mg; Carbohydrates: 67g; Fiber: 4g; Protein: 26g

Pizza Zucchini Boats

Zucchini boats are a simple, delicious way to add veggies to your lunch. Feel free to change up the toppings to suit your mood and taste buds. I like them with turkey pepperoni, which adds a zesty flavor that pairs well with the smoothness of the zucchini.

GLUTEN-FREE, 30 MINUTES OR LESS

PREP TIME: 10 minutes
COOK TIME: 10 minutes
SERVES 4
TEMPERATURE: 350°F

2 medium zucchini
Extra-virgin olive oil, for spraying
8 tablespoons pizza sauce
8 tablespoons shredded mozzarella cheese
½ cup mini turkey pepperoni
4 tablespoons shredded Parmesan cheese

1. Preheat the air fryer to 350°F.

2. Cut the zucchini in half lengthwise and scoop out the middles to create boats.

3. Lightly spray the zucchini with oil. Spoon 2 tablespoons pizza sauce into each boat. Sprinkle 2 tablespoons mozzarella on top of the pizza sauce. Top each boat with 6 or 7 mini pepperoni.

4. Lightly spray the air fryer basket with oil. Arrange the zucchini boats in a single layer in the basket.

5. Air fry for 6 to 8 minutes.

6. Sprinkle each boat with 1 tablespoon Parmesan cheese and serve.

Variation: You can make these zucchini boats vegetarian by removing the pepperoni and the Parmesan cheese.

PER SERVING: Calories: 179; Total fat: 10g; Saturated fat: 4g; Cholesterol: 42mg; Sodium: 893mg; Carbohydrates: 7g; Fiber: 2g; Protein: 16g

CHAPTER 4

Appetizers

Roasted Shishito Peppers

This simple four-ingredient appetizer will fly off the platter. These mild, sweet, and slightly smoky peppers are addictive when roasted in the air fryer. They taste great alone or served with a variety of dips or sauces, like creamy dill or roasted garlic aioli.

DAIRY-FREE, GLUTEN-FREE, VEGAN, 30 MINUTES OR LESS

PREP TIME: 5 minutes
COOK TIME: 10 minutes
SERVES 2 OR 3
TEMPERATURE: 400°F

1 (8-ounce) bag shishito peppers, whole, rinsed and dried
1 tablespoon avocado oil, plus more for the basket
1 tablespoon minced garlic
Salt

1. Preheat the air fryer to 400°F.

2. In a medium bowl, toss the shishitos with the avocado oil, garlic, and salt to taste.

3. Lightly spray the air fryer basket with oil. Place the shishitos in the basket.

4. Air fry for 8 to 10 minutes, shaking the basket every 3 to 4 minutes to ensure even cooking. The peppers should be roasted and blistered, but not burned.

PER SERVING: Calories: 105; Total fat: 7g; Saturated fat: 1g; Cholesterol: 0mg; Sodium: <1mg; Carbohydrates: 8g; Fiber: 5g; Protein: 3g

Vegetable Dumplings with Dipping Sauce

These homemade veggie-packed dumplings make a light and tasty appetizer for any gathering. The dipping sauce, which is a must, is also good for egg rolls. You might want to consider making a double batch because they tend to go quickly!

VEGETARIAN

PREP TIME: 30 minutes
COOK TIME: 20 minutes
SERVES 4
TEMPERATURE: 370°F

For the dumplings

1 tablespoon extra-virgin olive oil, plus more for spraying
1 (8-ounce) box cremini mushrooms, finely chopped
2 teaspoons minced garlic
1 teaspoon grated fresh ginger
1 (14-ounce) bag coleslaw mix, refrigerated
1 (12-ounce) package round dumpling wrappers

For the dipping sauce

1 tablespoon soy sauce
2 teaspoons rice vinegar
1 teaspoon sesame oil
½ tablespoon packed brown sugar

To make the dumplings

1. Heat the olive oil in a 10-inch skillet over medium heat. Add the mushrooms, garlic, and ginger and sauté for 2 to 3 minutes. Add the coleslaw mix and sauté for an additional 4 to 5 minutes, or until the coleslaw is soft. Stir the vegetables frequently and cook until all the moisture has evaporated and the mixture is dry.

2. Place 2 teaspoons of vegetable filling in the center of each dumpling wrapper.

3. Using your fingers or a pastry brush, moisten the edges of the dumpling wrapper with water. Fold over the wrapper and seal the edges with your fingers, making pleats and pinching the edges to close them well.

4. Preheat the air fryer to 370°F.

5. Lightly spray the air fryer basket with oil. Place the dumplings in a single layer in the basket. (Air fry in batches, if necessary.) Lightly spray with oil.

6. Air fry for 6 minutes. Flip the dumplings and lightly spray with oil. Air fry for an additional 6 minutes, or until golden brown and crispy.

To make the dipping sauce

7. While the dumplings are air frying, in a small bowl combine the soy sauce, rice vinegar, sesame oil, and brown sugar. Stir until the sugar dissolves.

8. Serve the dumplings with the dipping sauce.

Variation: To make this recipe vegan and vegetarian, use vegan dumpling wrappers.

PER SERVING: Calories: 299; Total fat: 5g; Saturated fat: 1g; Cholesterol: 0mg; Sodium: 501mg; Carbohydrates: 56g; Fiber: 3g; Protein: 12g

Crispy Stuffed Olives

Fried olives are a unique crowd-pleasing appetizer. They taste great on their own, or you can serve them with blue cheese dressing, yum yum sauce, or any other dipping sauce you have on hand. If you are lucky enough to have leftovers, you can reheat them in the air fryer in just 2 minutes for a delicious snack.

DAIRY-FREE, VEGETARIAN,
30 MINUTES OR LESS

PREP TIME: 15 minutes
COOK TIME: 10 minutes
SERVES 6
TEMPERATURE: 400°F

1 (10-ounce) jar garlic- or pimento-stuffed olives
¼ cup all-purpose flour
1 large egg
1 cup Italian seasoned panko bread crumbs
Extra-virgin olive oil, for spraying

1. Preheat the air fryer to 400°F.

2. Remove the olives from the jar and dry them completely with paper towels.

3. Put the flour in a small shallow bowl.

4. In a second small shallow bowl, beat the egg.

5. Put the bread crumbs in a third small shallow bowl.

6. Toss the olives in the flour.

7. Coat each olive in the beaten egg, then in the breading.

8. Lightly spray the air fryer basket with oil. Place the coated olives in a single layer in the basket. Lightly spray with oil.

9. Air fry for 6 to 8 minutes, shaking the basket gently after 2 minutes to ensure even cooking.

10. Serve hot.

Variation: If you want to kick up the spice level, try using jalapeño-stuffed olives.

PER SERVING: Calories: 144; Total fat: 9g; Saturated fat: 2g; Cholesterol: 31mg; Sodium: 810mg; Carbohydrates: 11g; Fiber: 1g; Protein: 3g

Sweet and Spicy Bacon-Wrapped Smokies

The combination of brown sugar and cayenne pepper is remarkable and creates an appetizer that will be the hit of any party. Serve these tasty bites with decorative toothpicks for a fun look.

GLUTEN-FREE, DAIRY-FREE

PREP TIME: 20 minutes
COOK TIME: 15 minutes
SERVES 8
TEMPERATURE: 375°F

¾ cup packed light
   brown sugar
½ teaspoon cayenne pepper
½ teaspoon freshly ground
   black pepper
1 pound sliced bacon, each
   slice cut into thirds
1 (14-ounce) package
   little smokies
Extra-virgin olive oil, for
   the basket

1. Preheat the air fryer to 375°F.

2. In a small shallow bowl, combine the brown sugar, cayenne pepper, and black pepper.

3. Wrap a piece of bacon around each little smokie. Roll each wrapped smokie in the brown sugar mixture. Press on the mixture to ensure it adheres.

4. Lightly spray the air fryer basket with oil. Place the smokies seam-side down in a single layer in the basket.

5. Air fry for 10 to 15 minutes, or until the bacon is cooked to your preferred level of crispiness.

Air Frying Tip: The cook time will vary based on the thickness of the bacon. If you have trouble keeping the bacon around the cocktail sausage, you can secure it with a toothpick.

Variation: Turn up the heat on this recipe by doubling the cayenne pepper.

PER SERVING: Calories: 502; Total fat: 36g; Saturated fat: 12g; Cholesterol: 83mg; Sodium: 1,363mg; Carbohydrates: 23g; Fiber: <1g; Protein: 25g

Baked Raspberry Brie

This elegant appetizer literally oozes rich, smooth flavor. Brie is a French cheese here complemented perfectly with raspberries and puff pastry. Serve with your choice of crackers for a lovely addition to any party.

30 MINUTES OR LESS

PREP TIME: 15 minutes
COOK TIME: 15 minutes
SERVES 6
TEMPERATURE: 350°F

1 tablespoon
  all-purpose flour
1 puff pastry sheet, at room
  temperature
1 (8-ounce) Brie wheel,
  refrigerated
¼ cup raspberry preserves
2 tablespoons fresh
  raspberries
1 large egg
1 tablespoon water
Extra-virgin olive oil, for
  the basket

1. Preheat the air fryer to 350°F.

2. Dust your work surface with the flour, then roll out the puff pastry sheet.

3. Cut the rind off the Brie and discard it. Place the Brie in the center of the puff pastry sheet.

4. Spread the raspberry preserves on top of the Brie, then sprinkle the fresh raspberries on top.

5. Fold up the sides of the puff pastry around the Brie. Press the seams of the pastry together until they are closed.

6. In a small bowl, whisk together the egg and water. Brush the egg wash all over the top and sides of the puff pastry.

7. Generously spray the air fryer basket with oil. Place the pastry-enrobed Brie in the basket.

8. Air fry for 10 to 15 minutes, or until the pastry is golden brown and cooked through.

Air Frying Tip: The puff pastry will tend to stick to the crisper plate even when you spray it with oil. You can use an air fryer-specific parchment paper liner, if desired.

Variation: You can use any flavor of preserves in place of raspberry. Fresh fruit can be added to the top or left off.

PER SERVING: Calories: 519; Total fat: 34g; Saturated fat: 19g; Cholesterol: 73mg; Sodium: 516mg; Carbohydrates: 51g; Fiber: 2g; Protein: 14g

Toasted Ravioli

You can use any kind of fresh ravioli to make a delicious toasted treat at home, and turn a main course into a fantastic appetizer. These ravioli are just as tasty as the ones you can order at your favorite Italian restaurant.

30 MINUTES OR LESS

PREP TIME: 15 minutes
COOK TIME: 10 minutes
SERVES 6
TEMPERATURE: 380°F

2 large eggs
2 tablespoons milk
¼ cup all-purpose flour
¾ cup Italian bread crumbs
⅓ cup grated Parmesan cheese
1 teaspoon Italian seasoning
¼ teaspoon salt
¼ teaspoon freshly ground black pepper
1 (8-ounce) package fresh ravioli, refrigerated
Extra-virgin olive oil, for spraying
Marinara sauce, for serving (optional)

1. Preheat the air fryer to 380°F.

2. In a small shallow bowl, whisk together the eggs and milk.

3. In a second small shallow bowl, put the flour.

4. In a third small shallow bowl, combine the bread crumbs, Parmesan cheese, Italian seasoning, salt, and pepper.

5. Coat each ravioli in the flour, then in the egg wash, then in the bread crumb mixture.

6. Lightly spray the air fryer basket with oil. Place the ravioli in a single layer in the basket. Lightly spray with oil.

7. Air fry for 4 minutes. Flip the ravioli and lightly spray with oil. Air fry for an additional 3 to 4 minutes, or until golden brown and crispy.

8. Serve with marinara sauce, if using.

PER SERVING: Calories: 246; Total fat: 8g; Saturated fat: 3g; Cholesterol: 87mg; Sodium: 652mg; Carbohydrates: 30g; Fiber: 2g; Protein: 11g

Jalapeño Poppers

Jalapeño poppers are a perennial party favorite. They're a spicy, creamy finger food perfect for game day or holiday parties. You will love the way the peppers sear in the air fryer and acquire a nice crisp texture.

VEGETARIAN, 30 MINUTES OR LESS

PREP TIME: 15 minutes
COOK TIME: 10 minutes
SERVES 8
TEMPERATURE: 370°F

8 large jalapeños
8 ounces cream cheese, at
　room temperature
½ cup panko bread crumbs
½ cup shredded cheese,
　any variety
2 teaspoons dried parsley
½ teaspoon garlic powder
Extra-virgin olive oil, for
　the basket

1. Preheat the air fryer to 370°F.

2. Remove the stems from the jalapeños, then cut them in half lengthwise. Carefully remove the seeds and insides to create boats.

3. In a medium bowl, combine the cream cheese, bread crumbs, shredded cheese, parsley, and garlic powder.

4. Stuff each jalapeño half with the cream cheese mixture.

5. Lightly spray the air fryer basket with oil. Place the poppers in a single layer in the basket.

6. Air fry for 7 to 10 minutes, or until the cheese is bubbly and golden brown and the jalapeños have softened.

Variation: For a decadent twist, you can wrap bacon around the jalapeño poppers after you've stuffed them. You'll need to increase the cook time to 10 to 15 minutes, or until the bacon is cooked and crispy.

PER SERVING: Calories: 159; Total fat: 12g; Saturated fat: 7g; Cholesterol: 35mg; Sodium: 144mg; Carbohydrates: 9g; Fiber: 1g; Protein: 4g

Sausage and Cheese Balls

My family has always enjoyed Sausage and Cheese Balls, but after I started making them in the air fryer, they couldn't get enough! Baking mix produces an amazingly crispy dish that will disappear in minutes.

30 MINUTES OR LESS

PREP TIME: 10 minutes
COOK TIME: 15 minutes
SERVES 6
TEMPERATURE: 350°F

1 pound bulk pork sausage, regular or spicy
2 cups baking mix, such as Bisquick
3 cups shredded sharp cheddar cheese
Extra-virgin olive oil, for the basket

1. Preheat the air fryer to 350°F.

2. In a large bowl, combine the sausage, baking mix, and cheese. Use a 1-inch cookie scoop to form 1-inch balls. You should have 30 to 35 balls.

3. Generously spray the air fryer basket with oil. Place the sausage balls in a single layer in the basket.

4. Air fry for 10 to 15 minutes, shaking the basket every 5 minutes to ensure even cooking, until golden brown and crispy.

Air Frying Tip: The cheese will cause the balls to stick to the crisper plate, so be sure to spray it thoroughly with oil before air frying.

PER SERVING: Calories: 552; Total fat: 34g; Saturated fat: 14g; Cholesterol: 111mg; Sodium: 1,162mg; Carbohydrates: 31g; Fiber: 1g; Protein: 27g

Pizza Pinwheels

Pizza Pinwheels are a fun and easy recipe that's perfect for a cocktail party, an after-school snack, or game day. The flavors of pizza burst from between the layers of buttery crescent dough, and the air fryer imparts a wonderful crispy texture.

30 MINUTES OR LESS

PREP TIME: 10 minutes
COOK TIME: 10 minutes, plus 10 minutes to chill
SERVES 4
TEMPERATURE: 350°F

1 tablespoon flour
1 (8-ounce) can crescent
  dough, refrigerated
½ cup pizza sauce
½ cup mozzarella cheese
½ cup shredded
  Parmesan cheese
Extra-virgin olive oil, for
  the basket

1. Preheat the air fryer to 350°F.

2. Dust your work surface with flour, then roll out the sheet of crescent dough.

3. Spread the pizza sauce evenly over the crescent dough all the way to the edges. Sprinkle the mozzarella cheese and Parmesan cheese over top of the pizza sauce.

4. Roll up the dough into a long tube. Place the rolled tube in the freezer for about 10 minutes to make cutting easier.

5. Cut the dough roll into 1-inch slices.

6. Lightly spray the air fryer basket with oil. Place the pinwheel slices in a single layer in the basket. Allow about ½ inch between each because they will expand a little during cooking.

7. Air fry for 5 minutes. Shake the basket and air fry for an additional 2 to 5 minutes, or until golden brown and cooked through.

Variation: You can add other pizza toppings in step 3 before rolling up the dough, but make sure they are chopped into small pieces.

PER SERVING: Calories: 309; Total fat: 19g; Saturated fat: 8g; Cholesterol: 20mg; Sodium: 821mg; Carbohydrates: 26g; Fiber: 1g; Protein: 10g

Zesty Seasoned Pretzels

If you love bold flavors, these Zesty Seasoned Pretzels will not disappoint. Pretzels are even crispier after being air fried. Package them up in pretty glass jars tied with a ribbon for an easy and delicious homemade gift.

30 MINUTES OR LESS

PREP TIME: 5 minutes
COOK TIME: 10 minutes
SERVES 6
TEMPERATURE: 350°F

⅓ cup extra-virgin olive oil, plus more for the basket
8 ounces pretzel twists
1 (0.6 ounce) package zesty Italian dressing mix
1 teaspoon dried parsley
½ teaspoon cayenne pepper

1. Preheat the air fryer to 350°F.

2. In a large zip-top bag, combine the olive oil, pretzels, Italian dressing mix, parsley, and cayenne pepper. Seal the bag, then shake it to completely coat the pretzels with the oil and seasonings.

3. Lightly spray the air fryer basket with oil. Place the coated pretzels in the basket.

4. Air fry for 5 to 8 minutes, shaking the basket at least once while cooking.

5. Let the pretzels cool before serving. Store in an airtight container for up to 1 week.

Variation: You can use any seasoning combination you prefer. Try a package of dry ranch dressing mix or some Cajun seasoning. Cook times will remain the same.

PER SERVING: Calories: 263; Total fat: 14g; Saturated fat: 2g; Cholesterol: 0mg; Sodium: 501mg; Carbohydrates: 31g; Fiber: 1g; Protein: 4g

Southwestern Egg Rolls

This flavorful Southwestern-style filling with corn, black beans, and green chiles pairs perfectly with an ultra-crispy egg roll wrapper. These golden-brown delights taste great dipped in a Southwestern ranch dressing.

VEGETARIAN, 30 MINUTES OR LESS

PREP TIME: 15 minutes
COOK TIME: 10 minutes
SERVES 5
TEMPERATURE: 375°F

1 (15-ounce) can black beans, drained and rinsed
1 cup corn kernels, frozen or canned, drained
1 (4-ounce) can diced green chiles
2 cups shredded Colby-Jack cheese
1 teaspoon paprika
1 teaspoon chili powder
1 teaspoon salt
½ teaspoon ground cumin
½ teaspoon freshly ground black pepper
1 (12-ounce) package egg roll wrappers
Extra-virgin olive oil, for spraying

1. Preheat the air fryer to 375°F.

2. In a large bowl, combine the black beans, corn, green chiles, cheese, paprika, chili powder, salt, cumin, and pepper.

3. Place an egg roll wrapper on your work surface diagonally so it looks like a diamond. Put about ¼ cup of filling onto the center of the wrapper. Fold the bottom corner over the filling and roll up snugly halfway to cover the filling. Fold in both sides of the wrapper. Moisten the edges of the top corner with water, roll up the rest of the way, and seal the top corner.

4. Repeat steps 2 and 3 with the remaining ingredients.

5. Lightly spray the air fryer basket with oil. Place the egg rolls seam-side down in the basket, leaving at least ¼ inch between each to ensure even cooking. Lightly spray with oil.

6. Air fry for 4 minutes. Flip the egg rolls and lightly spray with oil. Air fry for an additional 4 to 6 minutes, or until golden brown and crispy.

PER SERVING: Calories: 466; Total fat: 15g; Saturated fat: 9g; Cholesterol: 42mg; Sodium: 1,246mg; Carbohydrates: 58g; Fiber: 7g; Protein: 24g

Buffalo Chicken Meatballs

Buffalo chicken wings are popular, but this leaner version is easier to eat and may become your new favorite! This recipe allows to you enjoy all the spicy, tangy flavor of buffalo sauce in minutes and without the mess.

30 MINUTES OR LESS

PREP TIME: 10 minutes
COOK TIME: 15 minutes
SERVES 4
TEMPERATURE: 350°F

1 pound ground chicken
½ cup panko bread crumbs
1 large egg
3 tablespoons buffalo
   sauce, divided
2 teaspoons minced garlic
1 teaspoon dry ranch
   dressing mix
½ teaspoon salt
½ teaspoon freshly ground
   black pepper
Extra-virgin olive oil, for
   the basket

1. Preheat the air fryer to 350°F.

2. In a large bowl, combine the chicken, bread crumbs, egg, 1 tablespoon buffalo sauce, garlic, ranch dressing mix, salt, and pepper.

3. Form the mixture into 1-inch meatballs. You should have about 20 meatballs.

4. Lightly spray the air fryer basket with oil. Place the meatballs in a single layer in the basket. (Air fry in batches, if necessary.)

5. Air fry for 6 minutes. Shake the basket and air fry for an additional 6 to 9 minutes, or until browned and cooked through.

6. Toss with the remaining 2 tablespoons buffalo sauce before serving.

PER SERVING: Calories: 236; Total fat: 12g; Saturated fat: 3g; Cholesterol: 139mg; Sodium: 548mg; Carbohydrates: 9g; Fiber: <1g; Protein: 22g

Onion Rings

Hot and crisp, salty and slightly sweet, Onion Rings are a traditional fried food that can be made healthier in the air fryer. This version is just as delicious as what you get at a restaurant.

VEGETARIAN, 30 MINUTES OR LESS

PREP TIME: 15 minutes
COOK TIME: 10 minutes
SERVES 6
TEMPERATURE: 380°F

2 large sweet onions
1 cup all-purpose flour
1 teaspoon baking powder
2 teaspoons salt, divided
2 large eggs
2 tablespoons milk
2 cups panko bread crumbs
1 teaspoon smoked paprika
½ teaspoon onion powder
½ teaspoon garlic powder
½ teaspoon freshly ground
  black pepper
Pinch cayenne pepper
Extra-virgin olive oil, for
  spraying

1. Cut the ends off the onions and peel off the skins. Slice into ¼-inch-thick rings and separate the rings.

2. In a small shallow bowl, combine the flour, baking powder, and 1 teaspoon salt.

3. In a second small shallow bowl, whisk together the eggs and milk.

4. In a third small shallow bowl, combine the bread crumbs, paprika, onion powder, garlic powder, black pepper, and cayenne pepper.

5. Preheat the air fryer to 380°F.

6. Coat the onions in the flour mixture, then in the egg mixture, then in the bread crumbs. Press on the bread crumbs to ensure they adhere.

7. Lightly spray the air fryer basket with oil. Place the onion rings in a single layer in the basket. Lightly spray with oil.

8. Air fry for 5 minutes. Gently flip the onion rings and lightly spray with oil. Air fry for an additional 5 minutes, or until golden brown and crispy.

Air Frying Tip: Silicone-tipped tongs make it easy to flip the onion rings.

PER SERVING: Calories: 222; Total fat: 2g; Saturated fat: 1g; Cholesterol: 63mg; Sodium: 935mg; Carbohydrates: 42g; Fiber: 3g; Protein: 8g

Lemon-Pepper Chicken Wings

Lemon-pepper seasoning and honey lend bright flavors to this lighter version of chicken wings that will appeal to everyone. These wings will become your new favorite for the big game party.

GLUTEN-FREE, 30 MINUTES OR LESS

PREP TIME: 10 minutes
COOK TIME: 15 minutes
SERVES 6
TEMPERATURE: 400°F

For the wings

2 pounds fresh bone-in chicken wings
1 tablespoon baking powder
2 teaspoons salt
Extra-virgin olive oil, for spraying

For the sauce

8 tablespoons butter, melted
1 tablespoon lemon-pepper seasoning
2 teaspoons honey

To make the wings

1. Preheat the air fryer to 400°F.

2. Pat the chicken wings dry with paper towels.

3. In a large zip-top bag, mix together the baking powder and salt. Add the chicken wings, seal the bag, and shake to coat evenly.

4. Lightly spray the air fryer basket with oil. Place the chicken wings in a single layer in the basket. (Air fry in batches, if necessary.) Lightly spray with oil.

5. Air fry for 7 minutes. Flip the wings and lightly spray with oil. Air fry for an additional 6 to 8 minutes, or until the wings are crispy and lightly browned and have reached an internal temperature of 165°F.

To make the sauce

6. While the wings are air frying, in a small bowl, whisk together the melted butter, lemon-pepper seasoning, and honey.

7. As soon as the wings are done, toss them in the lemon-pepper sauce to coat.

PER SERVING: Calories: 417; Total fat: 34g; Saturated fat: 15g; Cholesterol: 128mg; Sodium: 1,538mg; Carbohydrates: 3g; Fiber: <1g; Protein: 22g

Avocado Fries with Dipping Sauce

If you like avocados, you will love avocado fries. The key is to start with firm avocados. Ripe ones will not hold up well during the air frying process and will end up mushy and lackluster. These fries are great on their own, served alongside creamy Sriracha dip, or with nearly anything you'd usually pair with avocados.

VEGETARIAN, 30 MINUTES
OR LESS

PREP TIME: 20 minutes
COOK TIME: 10 minutes
SERVES 6
TEMPERATURE: 350°F

For the avocado fries

4 slightly underripe
   avocados, halved
   and pitted
1½ cups panko
   bread crumbs
¾ teaspoon freshly ground
   black pepper
1½ teaspoons paprika
¾ teaspoon salt
3 large eggs
Extra-virgin olive oil, for
   spraying

For the dipping sauce

½ cup sour cream
½ cup mayonnaise
2 to 3 teaspoons sriracha
½ teaspoon freshly
   squeezed lemon juice

To make the avocado fries

1. Preheat the air fryer to 350°F.

2. Carefully remove the skin from the avocados while leaving the flesh intact. Cut each avocado in half lengthwise into 5 to 6 slices. Set aside.

3. In a small shallow bowl, mix together the bread crumbs, pepper, paprika, and salt.

4. In a second small shallow bowl, whisk the eggs.

5. Coat each avocado slice in the eggs, then in the bread crumbs. Press on the bread crumbs to ensure they adhere.

6. Lightly spray the air fryer basket with oil. Place the avocado fries in a single layer in the basket. Lightly spray with oil.

7. Air fry for 3 to 4 minutes. Gently flip the fries and lightly spray with oil. Air fry for an additional 3 to 4 minutes, or until golden brown and crispy.

To make the dipping sauce

8. While they're cooking, in a small bowl, combine the sour cream, mayonnaise, sriracha, and lemon juice.

9. Serve with the fries immediately.

PER SERVING: Calories: 424; Total fat: 34g; Saturated fat: 7g; Cholesterol: 101mg; Sodium: 530mg; Carbohydrates: 25g; Fiber: 7g; Protein: 7g

Crab Rangoon

Skip the buffet! You can make amazing crab rangoon at home in the air fryer. They will turn out golden brown and crispy on the outside with a creamy filling inside.

30 MINUTES OR LESS

PREP TIME: 15 minutes
COOK TIME: 10 minutes
SERVES 6
TEMPERATURE: 350°F

8 ounces cream cheese, at room temperature
1 (6-ounce) white crabmeat, picked through and drained
1 teaspoon minced garlic
½ teaspoon soy sauce
½ teaspoon confectioners' sugar
½ teaspoon dried chives
1 (12- to 16-ounce) package wonton wrappers
Extra-virgin olive oil, for spraying

1. Preheat the air fryer to 350°F.

2. In a medium bowl, mix together the cream cheese, crabmeat, garlic, soy sauce, confectioners' sugar, and chives.

3. Lay out the wonton wrappers and place a heaping teaspoon of cream cheese in the center of each.

4. Dab a bit of water on the outer edges of the wrappers and fold the two ends together to form a small pocket. Pinch the edges tightly to seal.

5. Lightly spray the air fryer basket with oil. Place the crab rangoon in a single layer in the basket. Lightly spray with oil.

6. Air fry for 7 minutes, or until golden brown and crispy.

Variation: If you prefer your Crab Rangoon without the hint of sweetness, you can omit the confectioners' sugar.

PER SERVING: Calories: 313; Total fat: 14g; Saturated fat: 8g; Cholesterol: 70mg; Sodium: 205mg; Carbohydrates: 35g; Fiber: 1g; Protein: 11g

Fried Pickles

Have you ever had a fried pickle? If you haven't, you're in for a treat, and this version couldn't be easier. The zingy dill makes them fun and hard to resist. If you prefer a spicy snack, use spicy dill spears instead of regular. They taste great dipped in classic ranch dressing.

DAIRY-FREE, VEGETARIAN,
30 MINUTES OR LESS

PREP TIME: 15 minutes
COOK TIME: 15 minutes
SERVES 4
TEMPERATURE: 400°F

1 cup all-purpose flour
1 teaspoon paprika
1 large egg
1⅓ cups panko
   bread crumbs
1 (24-ounce) jar dill
   pickle spears
Extra-virgin olive oil, for
   spraying

1. Preheat the air fryer to 400°F.

2. In a small shallow bowl, combine the flour and paprika.

3. In a second small shallow bowl, whisk the egg.

4. Put the bread crumbs in a third small shallow bowl.

5. Pat the pickle spears dry with paper towels.

6. Coat each pickle spear in the flour mixture, then in the egg, then in the bread crumbs.

7. Lightly spray the air fryer basket with oil. Place the pickle spears in a single layer in the basket, leaving about ¼ inch of space between each to ensure even cooking. (Air fry in batches, if necessary.) Lightly spray with oil.

8. Air fry for 7 minutes. Gently flip the pickles and air fry for an additional 5 to 8 minutes, or until lightly browned and crispy.

PER SERVING: Calories: 206; Total fat: 2g; Saturated fat: <1g; Cholesterol: 41mg; Sodium: 1,128mg; Carbohydrates: 39g; Fiber: 2g; Protein: 7g

Parmesan-Asparagus Twists

This appetizer is so elegant: beautiful bright green spears are delicately wrapped in puff pastry and flavored with Parmesan and a hint of cayenne pepper. Serve before a dinner party or as a fun way to get the kids to eat their vegetables.

30 MINUTES OR LESS

PREP TIME: 15 minutes
COOK TIME: 10 minutes
SERVES 6
TEMPERATURE: 350°F

24 asparagus spears
1 tablespoon extra-virgin
   olive oil, plus more for
   the basket
¼ teaspoon salt
¼ teaspoon freshly ground
   black pepper
Flour, for dusting
1 sheet puff pastry, at room
   temperature
1 large egg
1 teaspoon water
½ cup grated
   Parmesan cheese
¼ teaspoon cayenne pepper

1. In a large bowl, combine the asparagus, olive oil, salt, and black pepper. Toss to coat.

2. Preheat the air fryer to 350°F.

3. Dust your work surface with flour, then unfold the puff pastry sheet. Cut the sheet in half lengthwise, then cut each half into thin strips about ½ inch wide. You will need 24 strips.

4. Wrap a pastry strip around each asparagus spear, leaving the tip free. Place the wrapped spears on a baking sheet.

5. In a small shallow bowl, whisk together the egg and water.

6. In a second small shallow bowl, combine the Parmesan cheese and cayenne pepper.

7. Brush each wrapped spear with the egg wash, then sprinkle with the cheese mixture. Press on the mixture to ensure it adheres.

8. Lightly spray the air fryer basket with oil. Place the twists in a single layer in the basket, leaving about ½ inch of space between each. (Air fry in batches, if necessary.)

9. Air fry for 10 minutes, shaking the basket once while cooking, until the pastry is lightly browned.

PER SERVING: Calories: 402; Total fat: 25g; Saturated fat: 12g; Cholesterol: 35mg; Sodium: 539mg; Carbohydrates: 44g; Fiber: 4g; Protein: 11g

Loaded Potato Skins

The air fryer does wonders with potato skins by turning them into a crunchy, crispy party with every bite. This version includes the classic toppings; feel free to mix it up, or set up a potato bar and let everyone choose their own.

GLUTEN-FREE

PREP TIME: 10 minutes
COOK TIME: 55 minutes, plus 5 minutes to cool
SERVES 6
TEMPERATURE: 400°F

Extra-virgin olive oil, for greasing the basket
6 medium russet potatoes, scrubbed
Salt
Freshly ground black pepper
6 slices cooked bacon, crumbled
1 cup shredded cheddar cheese
½ cup sour cream, for serving
3 scallions, thinly sliced, for serving

1. Preheat the air fryer to 400°F.

2. Lightly spray the air fryer basket with oil. Lightly spray the potatoes with oil and season with salt and pepper. Pierce each potato a few times with a fork. Place the potatoes in the basket.

3. Air fry for 30 to 40 minutes, until fork-tender. The cook time will depend on the size of the potatoes.

4. Set aside the potatoes for 5 to 10 minutes, or until cool enough to handle. Cut the potatoes in half lengthwise. Scoop out most of the insides, leaving about ¼ inch so the potato skins hold their shape and resemble a boat.

5. Season the inside of the potato skins with salt and pepper. Lightly spray with oil.

6. Lightly spray the air fryer basket with oil. Place the potato skins in a single layer in the basket, leaving about ¼ inch of space between each to ensure even cooking. (Air fry in batches, if necessary.)

7. Air fry for 8 to 10 minutes, until crispy and golden. Carefully sprinkle the bacon and cheese into each potato skin. Air fry for an additional 2 to 3 minutes, or until the cheese is melted and bubbly.

8. Top with sour cream and scallions before serving.

PER SERVING: Calories: 322; Total fat: 13g; Saturated fat: 7g; Cholesterol: 38mg; Sodium: 276mg; Carbohydrates: 41g; Fiber: 3g; Protein: 12g

Stuffed Mushroom Caps

A mushroom stuffed with creamy cheeses is a divine party food. The air fryer removes the excess moisture that is a common problem when baking mushrooms in the oven, and you'll get an even better texture as a result.

30 MINUTES OR LESS

PREP TIME: 15 minutes
COOK TIME: 10 minutes
SERVES 5
TEMPERATURE: 370°F

24 large cremini mushrooms
4 ounces cream cheese, at
    room temperature
½ cup shredded
    mozzarella cheese
¼ cup grated
    Parmesan cheese
¼ cup Italian seasoned
    bread crumbs
1 large egg
¼ teaspoon salt
¼ teaspoon freshly ground
    black pepper
¼ teaspoon onion powder
Dash hot sauce
Extra-virgin olive oil, for
    spraying

1. Clean the mushrooms gently with a damp paper towel and remove the stems.

2. In a medium bowl, use an electric mixer to combine the cream cheese, mozzarella cheese, Parmesan cheese, bread crumbs, egg, salt, pepper, onion powder, and hot sauce.

3. Preheat the air fryer to 370°F.

4. Spoon the cheese mixture into each mushroom, pressing the mixture into the mushrooms and leaving a little bit mounded over the top.

5. Lightly spray the air fryer basket with oil. Place the stuffed mushrooms in a single layer in the basket. (Air fry in batches, if necessary.) Lightly spray with oil.

6. Air fry for 7 to 10 minutes, or until both the mushrooms and the cheese have started to brown lightly on top.

PER SERVING: Calories: 205; Total fat: 14g; Saturated fat: 7g; Cholesterol: 70mg; Sodium: 468mg; Carbohydrates: 11g; Fiber: 1g; Protein: 11g

Bacon-Wrapped Jumbo Shrimp

Sometimes simple is best. In this case, you need only two ingredients to wow your guests. Shrimp and bacon are a decadent combination. You won't be able to eat just one!

DAIRY-FREE, GLUTEN-FREE,
30 MINUTES OR LESS

PREP TIME: 10 minutes
COOK TIME: 15 minutes
SERVES 6
TEMPERATURE: 375°F

1 pound sliced bacon
16 ounces jumbo shrimp, peeled and deveined, tails on
Extra-virgin olive oil, for the basket

1. Preheat the fryer to 375°F.

2. Cut the bacon strips in half. Wrap half a strip tightly around each shrimp.

3. Lightly spray the air fryer basket with oil. Place each bacon-wrapped shrimp seam-side down in the basket.

4. Air fry for 12 to 15 minutes, or until the bacon is crispy and cooked to your preference. I like to check the progress after about 6 minutes and move the shrimp around a little so they don't stick to the basket.

Variation: This recipe is extremely simple and allows the flavors of the shrimp and bacon to shine. If you want to add more flavor, season the shrimp with salt and pepper or any way you like before wrapping with the bacon.

PER SERVING: Calories: 407; Total fat: 27g; Saturated fat: 9g; Cholesterol: 158mg; Sodium: 1,820mg; Carbohydrates: 1g; Fiber: 0g; Protein: 34g

Sticky Boneless Chicken "Wings" with Hoisin

These sweet and spicy chicken "wings" are actually tenderloins cut into bite-size pieces. They are juicy on the inside and crispy on the outside, and the sauce is the perfect combination of sweet and spicy.

DAIRY-FREE, 30 MINUTES
OR LESS

PREP TIME: 15 minutes
COOK TIME: 15 minutes
SERVES 4
TEMPERATURE: 390°F

For the chicken

2 large eggs
¾ cup all-purpose flour
1 teaspoon seasoned salt
½ teaspoon freshly ground
   black pepper
1 pound boneless chicken
   tenderloins, cut into thirds
Extra-virgin olive oil, for
   spraying

For the sauce

1 cup hoisin sauce
2 tablespoons sriracha
1 teaspoon fresh
   minced ginger

To make the chicken

1. Preheat the air fryer to 390°F.

2. In a small shallow bowl, beat the eggs.

3. In a second small shallow bowl, combine the flour, seasoned salt, and pepper.

4. Coat each chicken piece in the egg, then coat in the flour mixture.

5. Lightly spray the air fryer basket with oil. Place the coated chicken in the basket and lightly spray with oil.

6. Air fry for 6 minutes. Flip the chicken and lightly spray with oil. Air fry for an additional 5 to 10 minutes, or until the chicken is lightly browned and has reached an internal temperature of 165°F.

To make the sauce

7. While the chicken is cooking, in a medium bowl, combine the hoisin sauce, sriracha, and ginger.

8. Transfer the cooked chicken to the bowl and toss it in the sauce to coat. Serve hot.

PER SERVING: Calories: 371; Total fat: 5g; Saturated fat: 1g; Cholesterol: 129mg; Sodium: 1,800mg; Carbohydrates: 49g; Fiber: 3g; Protein: 30g

Creamy Crab Dip

This creamy dip is loaded with lump crabmeat and tiny shrimp. As an appetizer, it packs a punch of flavor, and the leftovers are great reheated or eaten cold. Serve with your choice of crackers, chips, or French bread.

30 MINUTES OR LESS

PREP TIME: 10 minutes
COOK TIME: 15 minutes
SERVES 6
TEMPERATURE: 325°F

1 (8-ounce) package cream cheese, at room temperature
1 cup mayonnaise
1½ teaspoons Old Bay seasoning
½ teaspoon ground mustard
1 (6-ounce) can lump crabmeat, drained and picked through
1 (4-ounce) can tiny shrimp, drained
¼ cup mozzarella cheese

1. Preheat the air fryer to 325°F.

2. In a medium bowl, combine the cream cheese, mayonnaise, Old Bay, and ground mustard.

3. Gently stir in the crabmeat, tiny shrimp, and mozzarella cheese.

4. Spoon the mixture into an oven-safe dish that will fit in the air fryer basket. Place the dish in the basket.

5. Air fry for 10 to 15 minutes, or until the top is golden brown and the dip is heated through.

6. Cover any leftovers and refrigerate for up to 3 days.

Air Frying Tip: Round cake pans come in many sizes and work very well for heated dips in the air fryer. Find cake pans that will fit in your air fryer basket to use for this dish and many other recipes.

PER SERVING: Calories: 430; Total fat: 42g; Saturated fat: 13g; Cholesterol: 125mg; Sodium: 796mg; Carbohydrates: 3g; Fiber: 0g; Protein: 11g

Garlicky Potato Wedges

These garlicky potato wedges turn out nice and crispy when cooked in the air fryer. They are a great appetizer or a perfect side dish for Classic Hamburgers (page 135) or Ranch-Bacon-Cheddar Sliders (page 142). Dip them in ketchup, fry sauce, or even ranch dressing.

GLUTEN-FREE, 30 MINUTES OR LESS

PREP TIME: 15 minutes
COOK TIME: 15 minutes
SERVES 6
TEMPERATURE: 360°F

6 medium russet potatoes, scrubbed
¼ cup extra-virgin olive oil, plus more for spraying
2 teaspoons minced garlic
2 teaspoons dried parsley
1 teaspoon onion powder
1 teaspoon salt
1 teaspoon paprika
½ teaspoon freshly ground black pepper
⅓ cup grated Parmesan cheese

1. Preheat the air fryer to 360°F.

2. Cut each potato in half lengthwise. Then cut them in half lengthwise again. Repeat until you have 8 wedges. Repeat for each potato.

3. In a large bowl, combine the olive oil, garlic, parsley, onion powder, salt, paprika, and pepper. Add the potatoes to the bowl and toss to coat. Sprinkle the Parmesan cheese on the potatoes and toss to coat evenly.

4. Lightly spray the air fryer basket with oil. Place the potato wedges in a single layer in the basket. Do not overcrowd.

5. Air fry for 15 minutes, flipping the potatoes halfway through. If you like your potatoes extra crunchy, lightly spray with oil when you flip them.

Variation: You can leave the Parmesan cheese out of this recipe to make it vegan.

PER SERVING: Calories: 276; Total fat: 11g; Saturated fat: 2g; Cholesterol: 5mg; Sodium: 504mg; Carbohydrates: 40g; Fiber: 3g; Protein: 6g

Eggplant Chips

It is always nice to have a healthy appetizer recipe on hand. These Eggplant Chips are a delicious, guilt-free alternative to traditional chips. Serve with marinara or a Greek yogurt dip.

DAIRY-FREE, GLUTEN-FREE, VEGAN

PREP TIME: 10 minutes
COOK TIME: 25 minutes
SERVES 4
TEMPERATURE: 330°F

½ teaspoon garlic powder
½ teaspoon chili powder
½ teaspoon dried oregano
½ teaspoon salt
1 large eggplant, sliced into ¼-inch rounds
1 tablespoon extra-virgin olive oil, plus more for the basket

1. Preheat the air fryer to 330°F.

2. In a small bowl, combine the garlic powder, chili powder, oregano, and salt.

3. In a large bowl, combine the eggplant slices, olive oil, and the spice mixture and toss to coat evenly.

4. Lightly spray the air fryer basket with oil. Place the eggplant slices in a single layer in the basket. Do not overcrowd. (Air fry in batches, if necessary.)

5. Air fry for 20 to 25 minutes, flipping the eggplant slices halfway through, until slightly crispy.

6. Transfer the eggplant chips to a wire rack. They will continue to crisp up as they cool.

Variation: Add some cayenne pepper to the spice mix if you want to kick up the heat on these chips.

PER SERVING: Calories: 76; Total fat: 4g; Saturated fat: 1g; Cholesterol: 0mg; Sodium: 13mg; Carbohydrates: 11g; Fiber: 5g; Protein: 2g

CHAPTER 5

Poultry

Garlic Turkey Burgers

Ground turkey is lower in saturated fat than ground beef and typically costs less, too. This moist burger is full of garlicky flavor. Serve these burgers with your favorite condiments and toppings. If you want a lower-carb meal, wrap the patties in large lettuce leaves instead of using buns.

DAIRY-FREE

PREP TIME: 10 minutes, plus 15 minutes to chill

COOK TIME: 20 minutes

SERVES 4

TEMPERATURE: 370°F

1 pound ground turkey
½ cup bread crumbs
1 tablespoon Dijon mustard
1 tablespoon Worcestershire sauce
1 tablespoon minced garlic
1 teaspoon sriracha
1 large egg
Salt
Freshly ground black pepper
Extra-virgin olive oil, for the basket
4 hamburger buns

1. In a large bowl, combine the turkey, bread crumbs, mustard, Worcestershire sauce, garlic, sriracha, and egg. The mixture will be sticky.

2. Form the meat mixture into four equal patties, then place them on a baking sheet. Refrigerate for 15 minutes.

3. Preheat the air fryer to 370°F. Season the turkey burgers with salt and pepper to taste.

4. Lightly spray the air fryer basket with oil. Place the turkey burgers in a single layer in the basket.

5. Air fry for 10 minutes. Flip the turkey burgers and air fry for an additional 6 to 10 minutes, or until the burgers are lightly browned and cooked through, and the internal temperature has reached 165°F.

6. Assemble the turkey burgers on the buns and serve.

Variation: If you prefer sliders, make 8 small patties and serve on slider buns.

PER SERVING: Calories: 406; Total fat: 18g; Saturated fat: 5g; Cholesterol: 129mg; Sodium: 566mg; Carbohydrates: 33g; Fiber: 2g; Protein: 27g

Chicken Florentine Meatballs

These juicy chicken meatballs are lower in calories than traditional beef and pork meatballs but are no less versatile. You can serve them with pasta and marinara or on subs, or they are wonderful as a main dish paired with a Caesar salad and Twisted Parmesan Breadsticks (page 210).

PREP TIME: 10 minutes
COOK TIME: 20 minutes
SERVES 4
TEMPERATURE: 350°F

1 pound ground chicken
2 large eggs, beaten
½ cup spinach, cooked and chopped with the water squeezed out
½ cup shredded Parmesan cheese
½ cup panko bread crumbs
1 tablespoon minced garlic
½ teaspoon salt
½ teaspoon freshly ground black pepper
Extra-virgin olive oil, for greasing the basket

1. Preheat the air fryer to 350°F.

2. In a large bowl, combine the chicken, eggs, spinach, Parmesan cheese, bread crumbs, garlic, salt, and pepper.

3. Use a 1-inch cookie scoop to form meatballs. You should have 20 to 25 meatballs.

4. Lightly spray the air fryer basket with oil. Place the meatballs in a single layer in the basket, leaving about ¼ inch between each to ensure even cooking. (Air fry in batches, if necessary.)

5. Air fry for 15 to 20 minutes, shaking the basket after 5 minutes, until golden brown and cooked through.

Air Frying Tip: It is important to squeeze all the water out of the cooked spinach so the meatball mixture isn't too wet. For extra crispy meatballs, lightly spray the meatballs with oil before air frying.

PER SERVING: Calories: 278; Total fat: 14g; Saturated fat: 5g; Cholesterol: 187mg; Sodium: 579mg; Carbohydrates: 9g; Fiber: <1g; Protein: 27g

Honey-Ginger Turkey Tenderloin

Turkey tenderloin is a lean and healthy white meat. Giving the tenderloin time to marinate will add a marvelous depth of flavor to this dish. Slice the turkey into strips after it is cooked and add it to a salad for a light meal, or serve it with Crispy Brussels Sprouts with Almonds (page 181) or Baby Potatoes (page 186) for a more traditional dinner.

DAIRY-FREE, GLUTEN-FREE

PREP TIME: 5 minutes, plus up to 4 hours to marinate and 10 minutes to rest

COOK TIME: 30 minutes

SERVES 4

TEMPERATURE: 370°F

3 tablespoons honey

3 tablespoons soy sauce

3 tablespoons balsamic vinegar

2 teaspoons minced garlic

1 teaspoon grated fresh ginger

2 teaspoons extra-virgin olive oil, plus more for the basket

1½ pounds turkey tenderloin

1. In a small bowl, whisk together the honey, soy sauce, balsamic vinegar, garlic, ginger, and olive oil.

2. Reserve 2 tablespoons of the marinade. Pour the remaining marinade into a large zip-top bag and add the turkey tenderloin. Make sure the tenderloin is completely coated. Seal the bag, place it in the refrigerator, and let it marinate for at least 1 hour or up to 4 hours.

3. Preheat the air fryer to 370°F.

4. Lightly spray the air fryer basket with oil. Place the marinated tenderloin in the basket.

5. Air fry for 15 minutes. Flip the tenderloin and lightly spray with oil. Air fry for an additional 10 to 15 minutes, or until the tenderloin reaches an internal temperature of at least 165°F.

6. Top with the reserved marinade and let the meat rest for 10 minutes before slicing and serving.

Air Frying Tip: If you have a small air fryer, you can cut the tenderloin into 2 or 3 pieces so it will fit in the basket.

PER SERVING: Calories: 268; Total fat: 3g; Saturated fat: <1g; Cholesterol: 105mg; Sodium: 743mg; Carbohydrates: 16g; Fiber: <1g; Protein: 43g

Chicken Parmesan

Home-cooked Italian food makes mealtime special. I love how crisp the cutlet gets in this recipe. It provides a perfect contrast with the soft melted cheese on top. It's delicious served with salad and Cheesy Garlic Bread (page 214).

30 MINUTES OR LESS

PREP TIME: 15 minutes
COOK TIME: 10 minutes
SERVES 4
TEMPERATURE: 350°F

2 boneless, skinless
  chicken breasts
1 large egg
½ cup bread crumbs
¼ cup grated
  Parmesan cheese
1 teaspoon Italian seasoning
Extra-virgin olive oil, for
  spraying
½ cup marinara sauce
1 cup shredded
  mozzarella cheese

1. Slice the chicken breasts in half lengthwise to get 4 thinly sliced cutlets. Using a meat mallet, lightly pound the thicker area of the breast to even out the thickness.

2. In a small shallow bowl, whisk the egg.

3. In a second small shallow bowl, combine the bread crumbs, Parmesan cheese, and Italian seasoning.

4. Preheat the air fryer to 350°F.

5. Coat each chicken cutlet in the egg, then in the bread crumb mixture.

6. Lightly spray the air fryer basket with oil. Place the coated cutlets in a single layer in the basket. (Air fry in batches, if necessary.) Lightly spray with oil.

7. Air fry for 6 minutes. Flip the cutlets and spoon 2 tablespoons marinara sauce on top of each. Sprinkle with about ¼ cup mozzarella cheese and press on the cheese to ensure it adheres.

8. Air fry for an additional 4 minutes, or until the cheese has melted and started to crisp.

Air Frying Tip: Thin pieces of meat will cook quickly in the air fryer. Using a meat mallet helps get the meat to an even thickness so it cooks evenly.

PER SERVING: Calories: 250; Total fat: 10g; Saturated fat: 4g; Cholesterol: 106mg; Sodium: 516mg; Carbohydrates: 16g; Fiber: 1g; Protein: 23g

Jalapeño Popper Chicken Meatballs

The flavors of jalapeño poppers inside a meatball may surprise you. If you like some extra heat, do not deseed the jalapeños. Try these addictive meatballs in a rich chicken broth or served with Loaded Corn Fritters (page 180).

30 MINUTES OR LESS

PREP TIME: 10 minutes
COOK TIME: 15 minutes
SERVES 4
TEMPERATURE: 350°F

1 pound ground chicken
¼ cup bread crumbs
¼ cup shredded
   Parmesan cheese
3 tablespoons crumbled
   cooked bacon
2 ounces cream cheese, at
   room temperature
1 medium jalapeño, seeded
   and finely diced
1 teaspoon garlic powder
½ teaspoon onion powder
Extra-virgin olive oil, for
   spraying

1. Preheat the air fryer to 350°F.

2. In a large bowl, combine the chicken, bread crumbs, Parmesan cheese, bacon, cream cheese, jalapeño, garlic powder, and onion powder.

3. Use a 1-inch small cookie scoop to form meatballs. You should have 20 to 25 meatballs.

4. Lightly spray the air fryer basket with oil. Place the meatballs in a single layer in the basket, leaving about ¼ inch between each to ensure even cooking. (Air fry in batches, if necessary.) Lightly spray with oil.

5. Air fry for 12 to 15 minutes, shaking the basket after 5 minutes, until golden brown and cooked through.

Variation: If you do not care for the crunch of fresh jalapeños, you can dice pickled jalapeños, but be sure to pat them dry with paper towels before adding them to the meat mixture.

PER SERVING: Calories: 282; Total fat: 17g; Saturated fat: 7g; Cholesterol: 119mg; Sodium: 311mg; Carbohydrates: 7g; Fiber: 1g; Protein: 25g

Spicy Chicken Bites

These chicken bites are not only spicy, they're also sweet. The brown sugar and spice mixture caramelizes on each piece for irresistible flavor. Eat these bites on their own for a light meal or add them to a large salad.

DAIRY-FREE, GLUTEN-FREE, 30 MINUTES OR LESS

PREP TIME: 15 minutes
COOK TIME: 10 minutes
SERVES 4
TEMPERATURE: 390°F

½ cup light brown sugar
1 tablespoon paprika
½ tablespoon garlic powder
1 teaspoon ground
   red pepper
½ teaspoon salt, plus more
   for seasoning
¼ teaspoon freshly ground
   black pepper, plus more
   for seasoning
2 boneless, skinless
   chicken breasts
Extra-virgin olive oil, for
   the basket

1. In a small bowl, combine the brown sugar, paprika, garlic powder, red pepper, salt, and black pepper.

2. Cut the chicken breasts into 1-inch chunks and season with salt and black pepper.

3. Preheat the air fryer to 390°F.

4. Coat the chicken pieces all over with the seasoning mixture.

5. Lightly spray the air fryer basket with oil. Place the coated chicken in a single layer in the basket.

6. Air fry for 5 minutes. Shake the basket and air fry for an additional 3 to 5 minutes, or until the chicken is cooked through and the outside is crispy and caramelized.

Variation: For a fun twist, you can wrap one-third of a slice of bacon around each piece of chicken before coating in the seasoning mixture, then cook until the bacon is nice and crispy.

PER SERVING: Calories: 144; Total fat: 2g; Saturated fat: <1g; Cholesterol: 40mg; Sodium: 327mg; Carbohydrates: 20g; Fiber: 1g; Protein: 13g

Spiced Cornish Game Hens

Looking to try a new poultry dish for dinner? Cornish game hens are a wonderful option for a weekend dinner or for entertaining guests, and they are amazingly simple to cook in the air fryer. These look lovely on a platter, served alongside Lemon-Garlic Green Beans and Mushrooms (page 179).

DAIRY-FREE, GLUTEN-FREE

PREP TIME: 10 minutes
COOK TIME: 40 minutes, plus 10 minutes to rest
SERVES 4
TEMPERATURE: 370°F

2 frozen Cornish game
  hens, thawed
Extra-virgin olive oil, for
  spraying
Salt
Freshly ground black pepper
½ cup frozen orange juice
  concentrate, thawed
¼ cup honey
¼ cup ketchup
1 to 2 teaspoons cornstarch
Dash hot sauce

1. Preheat the air fryer to 370°F.

2. Lightly spray the game hens with oil and season all over with salt and pepper.

3. Lightly spray the air fryer basket with oil. Place the hens in a single layer in the basket.

4. Air fry for 15 minutes. Flip the hens and air fry for an additional 15 minutes.

5. Meanwhile, in a small saucepan, combine the orange juice concentrate, honey, ketchup, 1 teaspoon cornstarch, and hot sauce. Bring to a boil and cook for about 5 minutes, or until it reaches a syrup consistency. Add the remaining 1 teaspoon cornstarch if the consistency is too thin.

6. Flip the hens again and use a pastry brush to baste them with the marinade. Air fry for 5 minutes. Flip the hens one more time and baste again. Air fry for an additional 5 minutes, or until the skin is crispy and the hens reach an internal temperature of 165°F.

7. Let the hens rest for 10 minutes before carving and serving.

PER SERVING: Calories: 467; Total fat: 24g; Saturated fat: 7g; Cholesterol: 170mg; Sodium: 242mg; Carbohydrates: 34g; Fiber: <1g; Protein: 30g

Green Chile-Turkey Muffins

These muffins are a fun protein option for a quick weeknight dinner. Each one is like a mini meat loaf packed with the flavors of the Southwest. Serve with Loaded Corn Fritters (page 180) or Twice-Baked Potatoes (page 192).

PREP TIME: 10 minutes
COOK TIME: 15 minutes
SERVES 4
TEMPERATURE: 350°F

1 large egg, beaten
1 pound ground turkey
1 cup shredded Mexican blend cheese
¾ cup bread crumbs
¼ cup salsa verde
1 (4-ounce) can diced green chiles
2 teaspoons minced garlic
1 teaspoon chili powder
1 teaspoon onion powder
½ teaspoon ground cumin
¼ teaspoon salt
¼ teaspoon freshly ground black pepper

1. Preheat the air fryer to 350°F.

2. In a large bowl, combine the egg, turkey, cheese, bread crumbs, salsa verde, green chiles, garlic, chili powder, onion powder, cumin, salt, and pepper. Mix gently until well combined.

3. Fill 12 to 14 silicone muffin cups with the turkey mixture until each is three-quarters full.

4. Place the muffin cups in the air fryer basket.

5. Air fry for 12 to 16 minutes, or until the tops are browned and crispy and the internal temperature has reached 165°F.

Air Frying Tip: These muffins will slide right out of the silicone muffin cups—no need to spray with oil. Cook times can vary based on how much meat you put in each muffin cup.

PER SERVING: Calories: 434; Total fat: 26g; Saturated fat: 10g; Cholesterol: 154mg; Sodium: 829mg; Carbohydrates: 20g; Fiber: 2g; Protein: 31g

Honey-Balsamic Turkey Breast

Turkey breast is delicious and can be enjoyed year-round—not just on the holidays. The honey-balsamic glaze makes all the difference in this dish, and you will be shocked at how tender and juicy the meat is. A 3-pound turkey breast is big enough to serve 6 to 8 people. If you have leftovers, rejoice! You'll be able to enjoy a fantastic turkey sandwich for lunch tomorrow.

DAIRY-FREE, GLUTEN-FREE

PREP TIME: 10 minutes, plus 20 minutes to marinate

COOK TIME: 40 minutes, plus 10 minutes to rest

SERVES 8

TEMPERATURE: 370°F

⅓ cup pulp-free orange juice

3½ tablespoons honey

1½ tablespoons balsamic vinegar

1½ tablespoons Dijon mustard

½ teaspoon salt

¼ teaspoon freshly ground black pepper

1 (3-pound) frozen turkey breast, thawed and trimmed of fat

1. In a medium bowl, whisk together the orange juice, honey, balsamic vinegar, mustard, salt, and pepper. Measure out ¼ cup of marinade and set aside.

2. Place the turkey breast in the bowl of marinade and turn so it is thoroughly coated. Cover the bowl and refrigerate for 20 minutes, flipping the turkey breast halfway through.

3. Preheat the air fryer to 370°F.

4. Wrap the turkey in aluminum foil and place it in the air fryer basket.

5. Air fry for 20 minutes.

6. Remove the foil from the turkey and spray the basket with oil. Using a pastry brush, baste the turkey with the some of the reserved marinade. Air fry for 10 minutes. Flip the turkey breast and baste again. Air fry for an additional 10 minutes, or until the internal temperature has reached 165°F.

7. Let the turkey rest for 10 minutes before slicing and serving.

Air Frying Tip: Wrapping the thick turkey breast in foil allows time for the inside to cook before the outside crisps up.

PER SERVING: Calories: 263; Total fat: 11g; Saturated fat: 3g; Cholesterol: 90mg; Sodium: 816mg; Carbohydrates: 11g; Fiber: <1g; Protein: 30g

General Tso's Chicken

You will not have any regrets about skipping takeout after you make this version of a restaurant favorite in your air fryer. This tangy, sweet, and crispy chicken can be ready in just 20 minutes. Serve with white rice for a delicious meal.

DAIRY-FREE, 30 MINUTES
OR LESS

PREP TIME: 5 minutes
COOK TIME: 10 minutes
SERVES 4
TEMPERATURE: 400°F

For the chicken

1 pound boneless, skinless
   chicken thighs, cut into
   1-inch pieces
2 tablespoons cornstarch
½ teaspoon salt
½ teaspoon freshly ground
   black pepper
Extra-virgin olive oil, for
   the basket

For the sauce

¼ cup chicken stock
1½ tablespoons tomato paste
1 tablespoon soy sauce
1 tablespoon rice vinegar
1 tablespoon sugar
1 teaspoon hoisin sauce
1 teaspoon chili paste
1 teaspoon sesame oil
1 teaspoon minced
   fresh ginger
1 teaspoon cornstarch

To make the chicken

1. Preheat the air fryer to 400°F.

2. In a medium bowl, toss the chicken pieces with the cornstarch, salt, and pepper until the pieces are evenly coated.

3. Lightly spray the air fryer basket with oil. Place the coated chicken in a single layer in the basket.

4. Air fry for 10 minutes, shaking the basket every 3 minutes, until the chicken is crispy and reaches an internal temperature of at least 165°F.

To make the sauce

5. While the chicken is cooking, in a small saucepan over low heat, combine the chicken stock, tomato paste, soy sauce, rice vinegar, sugar, hoisin sauce, chili paste, sesame oil, ginger, and cornstarch. Whisk the sauce until the sugar and cornstarch are dissolved. Bring to a boil, then reduce the heat to low and simmer for 5 to 7 minutes, or until the sauce thickens.

6. Toss the chicken in the sauce and serve.

Air Frying Tip: A light coating of cornstarch helps foods get crispier, eliminating the need for heavy breading.

PER SERVING: Calories: 186; Total fat: 8g; Saturated fat: <1g; Cholesterol: 91mg; Sodium: 758mg; Carbohydrates: 10g; Fiber: <1g; Protein: 19g

Whole Roasted Chicken

Roasting a whole chicken may sound difficult, but it's actually amazingly simple—especially in the air fryer. You can shred leftover chicken and use it in soups, salads, enchiladas, or wraps. Try doubling or tripling the spice mix and keeping it on hand, because this recipe is sure to become a regular in your menu rotation.

DAIRY-FREE, GLUTEN-FREE

PREP TIME: 15 minutes
COOK TIME: 1 hour, plus
10 minutes to rest
SERVES 6
TEMPERATURE: 360°F

2 teaspoons salt
1 teaspoon freshly ground
   black pepper
1 teaspoon paprika
½ teaspoon onion powder
½ teaspoon dried thyme
¼ teaspoon cayenne pepper
¼ teaspoon garlic powder
1 (4-pound) fryer chicken
Extra-virgin olive oil, for
   brushing and spraying

1. In a small bowl, combine the salt, black pepper, paprika, onion powder, thyme, cayenne pepper, and garlic powder.

2. Remove the giblets from the chicken. Using paper towels, pat the chicken dry as thoroughly as possible, including the cavity.

3. Preheat the air fryer to 360°F.

4. Brush the chicken thoroughly with oil and rub it with the seasoning mixture.

5. Truss the chicken or tie the legs with butcher's twine. (This step makes it easier to flip the chicken during cooking.)

6. Place the chicken breast-side down in the air fryer basket. Air fry for 30 minutes. Flip the chicken and baste it with any drippings collected in the bottom of the basket. Lightly spray with oil.

7. Air fry for an additional 20 minutes. Flip the chicken one last time and air fry for about 10 minutes, or until it is crispy and golden and a meat thermometer inserted into the thickest part of the thigh reaches an internal temperature of at least 165°F.

8. Let the chicken rest for 10 minutes before carving.

PER SERVING: Calories: 399; Total fat: 28g; Saturated fat: 8g; Cholesterol: 138mg; Sodium: 915mg; Carbohydrates: 1g; Fiber: <1g; Protein: 34g

Fajita Chicken Kebabs

These kebabs can be enjoyed right off the skewers, or you can remove the cooked chicken and veggies from the skewer and nestle them in a tortilla. For the latter, serve with shredded cheese, sour cream, and jalapeños, if desired.

DAIRY-FREE, GLUTEN-FREE

PREP TIME: 15 minutes, plus 4 hours to marinate

COOK TIME: 20 minutes

SERVES 6

TEMPERATURE: 350°F

2 tablespoons freshly squeezed lime juice

2 tablespoons freshly squeezed orange juice

1 tablespoon extra-virgin olive oil, plus more for spraying

1½ teaspoons paprika

1½ teaspoons garlic powder

½ teaspoon ancho chile powder

½ teaspoon salt

⅛ teaspoon ground cinnamon

1 pound boneless, skinless chicken breasts, cut into bite-size chunks

1 large white onion, cut into 1-inch chunks

2 bell peppers (red, yellow, or orange), cut into 1-inch chunks

1. In a large zip-top bag, combine the lime juice, orange juice, olive oil, paprika, garlic powder, chile powder, salt, and cinnamon.

2. Add the chicken chunks, seal the bag, and make sure all the chicken is covered with the marinade. Refrigerate the bag to marinate for 4 hours or overnight.

3. Preheat the air fryer to 350°F.

4. Thread the chicken, onion, and bell peppers in an alternating pattern onto 6-inch metal skewers.

5. Place the chicken kebabs in a single layer in the air fryer basket. (Air fry in batches, if necessary.)

6. Air fry for 10 minutes. Flip the kebabs and lightly spray with oil. Air fry for an additional 5 to 10 minutes, or until the chicken reaches an internal temperature of at least 165°F.

Variation: Add any vegetables to your kebabs that you have on hand. Zucchini, squash, and mushrooms are great options.

PER SERVING: Calories: 135; Total fat: 5g; Saturated fat: 1g; Cholesterol: 53mg; Sodium: 430mg; Carbohydrates: 7g; Fiber: 2g; Protein: 18g

Tuscan-Style Stuffed Chicken

These Tuscan-inspired stuffed chicken breasts are filled with creamy, cheesy goodness. The blend of cheeses with spices and spinach is lovely. Serve this delectable main dish with Baby Potatoes (page 186) and a simple green salad.

GLUTEN-FREE, 30 MINUTES OR LESS

PREP TIME: 15 minutes
COOK TIME: 15 minutes
SERVES 4
TEMPERATURE: 380°F

8 ounces cream cheese, at room temperature
¼ cup mozzarella cheese
¼ cup shredded Parmesan cheese
1 tablespoon minced garlic
5 ounces frozen chopped spinach, thawed, drained, and squeezed dry
½ teaspoon salt, plus more for seasoning
½ teaspoon freshly ground black pepper, plus more for seasoning
4 boneless, skinless chicken breasts
½ teaspoon paprika
Extra-virgin olive oil, for spraying

1. In a medium bowl, mix together the cream cheese, mozzarella cheese, Parmesan cheese, garlic, spinach, salt, and pepper.

2. Preheat the air fryer to 380°F.

3. Make 6 slits on the top of each chicken breast, going three-quarters of the way through, taking care not to cut completely through. Season with salt and pepper.

4. Fill the slots with the cream cheese mixture. Sprinkle with the paprika.

5. Lightly spray the air fryer basket with oil. Place the stuffed chicken breasts in a single layer in the basket. (Air fry in batches, if necessary.) Lightly spray with oil.

6. Air fry for 10 minutes. Spoon any leftover cream cheese mixture on top of the chicken and air fry for an additional 2 minutes, or until the chicken has reached an internal temperature of 165°F.

Air Frying Tip: It is important to squeeze all the water out of the frozen and thawed spinach so the filling isn't too wet.

PER SERVING: Calories: 386; Total fat: 26g; Saturated fat: 14g; Cholesterol: 147mg; Sodium: 684mg; Carbohydrates: 5g; Fiber: 1g; Protein: 33g

Rosemary-Lemon Chicken Thighs

Chicken thighs are incredibly versatile. The darker meat is tender and flavorful and will not dry out as quickly as chicken breasts. The rosemary-lemon marinade brings bright flavors to this simple yet versatile chicken dish, which you can serve with any number of sides, including Lemon-Garlic Green Beans and Mushrooms (page 179).

DAIRY-FREE, GLUTEN-FREE

PREP TIME: 5 minutes, plus 1 hour to marinate
COOK TIME: 15 minutes
SERVES 4
TEMPERATURE: 380°F

1 tablespoon freshly squeezed lemon juice
6 sprigs fresh rosemary, leaves removed and finely chopped
1 tablespoon extra-virgin olive oil, plus more for the basket
1 tablespoon minced garlic
1 teaspoon salt
½ teaspoon freshly ground black pepper
8 boneless, skinless chicken thighs

1. In a small bowl, combine the lemon juice, rosemary, olive oil, garlic, salt, and pepper.

2. Pour the marinade into a large zip-top bag and add the chicken. Seal the bag and refrigerate for 1 hour or up to overnight.

3. Preheat the air fryer to 380°F.

4. Lightly spray the air fryer basket with oil. Place the chicken smooth-side down in a single layer in the basket. (Air fry in batches, if necessary.) Lightly spray with oil.

5. Air fry for 8 minutes. Flip the chicken and lightly spray with oil. Air fry for an additional 4 minutes, or until the chicken is golden brown and has reached an internal temperature of 165°F.

PER SERVING: Calories: 296; Total fat: 17g; Saturated fat: 1g; Cholesterol: 180mg; Sodium: 910mg; Carbohydrates: 1g; Fiber: <1g; Protein: 36g

Chicken Piccata

This bright and tangy lemon-butter sauce poured over crispy chicken cutlets makes a delightful dinner. This healthier version pairs perfectly with Baby Potatoes (page 186) or roasted vegetables served on the side.

30 MINUTES OR LESS

PREP TIME: 10 minutes
COOK TIME: 10 minutes
SERVES 4
TEMPERATURE: 400°F

For the chicken
2 boneless, skinless
   chicken breasts
Salt
Freshly ground black pepper
1 large egg, beaten
1 tablespoon freshly
   squeezed lemon juice
½ cup panko bread crumbs
3 tablespoons grated
   Parmesan cheese
1 teaspoon Italian seasoning
Extra-virgin olive oil, for
   the basket

To make the chicken

1. Slice each chicken breast in half so you have 4 thinner cutlets. Place the cutlets between two sheets of parchment paper or plastic wrap. Using a meat mallet, pound into ¼-inch-thick cutlets. Season with salt and pepper on both sides.

2. In a small shallow bowl, whisk together the egg and lemon juice.

3. In a second small shallow bowl, combine the bread crumbs, Parmesan cheese, and Italian seasoning.

4. Preheat the air fryer to 400°F.

5. Coat each chicken cutlet in the egg mixture, then dredge in the breading.

6. Lightly spray the air fryer basket with oil. Place the coated cutlets in a single layer in the basket. (Air fry in batches, if necessary.) Lightly spray with oil.

7. Air fry for 4 minutes. Flip the cutlets and lightly spray with oil. Air fry for an additional 4 minutes, or until the chicken has reached an internal temperature of 165°F.

For the sauce

1 tablespoon butter

½ cup dry white wine

¼ cup freshly squeezed
  lemon juice

2 teaspoons minced garlic

1 teaspoon cornstarch

½ teaspoon salt

¼ teaspoon freshly ground
  black pepper

1 tablespoon
  capers, drained

To make the sauce

8. While the cutlets are cooking, in a small saucepan over low heat, combine the butter, wine, lemon juice, garlic, cornstarch, salt, and pepper. Whisk until the cornstarch has dissolved. Bring the mixture to a gentle boil, then reduce the heat to low and simmer for 5 to 7 minutes, or until the sauce has thickened slightly. Remove from the heat and stir in the capers.

9. Transfer the cutlets to a serving platter, pour the sauce over them, and serve.

PER SERVING: Calories: 200; Total fat: 7g; Saturated fat: 3g; Cholesterol: 98mg; Sodium: 511mg; Carbohydrates: 12g; Fiber: 1g; Protein: 17g

Buttermilk Chicken Tenders

Marinating chicken in buttermilk is a great way to tenderize the meat. These crispy chicken tenders are perfect for dipping in barbecue sauce, honey mustard, ranch dressing, or ketchup. Eat them as an appetizer or a main dish with Baby Potatoes (page 186) or Classic French Fries (page 191)—either way, you won't have any leftovers.

PREP TIME: 10 minutes, plus 1 hour to marinate

COOK TIME: 10 minutes

SERVES 4

TEMPERATURE: 380°F

¾ cup buttermilk

2 teaspoons minced garlic

1 teaspoon salt

1 pound chicken tenderloins

1½ cups panko bread crumbs

2 teaspoons dried parsley

1 teaspoon seasoned salt

Extra-virgin olive oil, for spraying

1. In a large zip-top bag, combine the buttermilk, garlic, salt, and chicken. Seal the bag and refrigerate for 1 hour or up to overnight.

2. In a small shallow bowl, combine the bread crumbs, parsley, and seasoned salt.

3. Preheat the air fryer to 380°F.

4. Remove the chicken from the marinade and let any excess drip off. Coat the tenderloins in the bread crumb mixture. Press the mixture to ensure it adheres.

5. Lightly spray the air fryer basket with oil. Place the chicken in a single layer in the basket. (Air fry in batches, if necessary.) Lightly spray with oil.

6. Air fry for 5 minutes. Flip the chicken tenders and lightly spray with oil. Air fry for an additional 5 minutes, or until the chicken is crispy and the internal temperature has reached 165°F.

Variation: If you do not have buttermilk on hand, you can make your own. Add 1 tablespoon of lemon juice or vinegar to 1 cup of whole or 2% milk. Let stand 10 minutes before using.

PER SERVING: Calories: 249; Total fat: 2g; Saturated fat: 1g; Cholesterol: 60mg; Sodium: 1,069mg; Carbohydrates: 25g; Fiber: 1g; Protein: 31g

Crispy Fried Chicken

Everyone loves fried chicken, but it's often fried in large quantities of oil. This crispy air-fried chicken is missing the excess of oil and the a heavy breaded coating; instead, the seasonings blend makes it light, crispy, and flavorful.

PREP TIME: 10 minutes, plus 1 hour to marinate
COOK TIME: 20 minutes
SERVES 4
TEMPERATURE: 380°F

1 whole skin-on chicken, cut into 8 pieces (reserve the wings for another use)
1½ cups buttermilk
2 teaspoons hot sauce
1 teaspoon salt, divided
2 cups all-purpose flour
2 teaspoons onion powder
2 teaspoons garlic powder
2 teaspoons paprika
½ teaspoon freshly ground black pepper
Extra-virgin olive oil, for spraying

1. Cut the breast pieces in half so you have smaller pieces.

2. In a large zip-top bag, combine the buttermilk, hot sauce, ½ teaspoon of salt, and chicken. Seal the bag and refrigerate for 1 hour or up to overnight.

3. In a small shallow bowl, combine the flour, onion powder, garlic powder, paprika, pepper, and remaining ½ teaspoon of salt.

4. Preheat the air fryer to 380°F.

5. Remove the chicken from the buttermilk mixture and let any excess drip off. Roll the chicken in the flour mixture until it is completely coated.

6. Lightly spray the air fryer basket with oil. Place the chicken in a single layer in the basket. (Air fry in batches, if necessary.) Lightly spray with oil.

7. Air fry for 8 minutes. Check the chicken and spray any dry flour spots with oil. Flip the chicken and spray generously with oil.

8. Air fry for an additional 8 minutes, or until the chicken is crispy and the internal temperature has reached 165°F. If the chicken has not reached the correct internal temperature, lightly spray with oil and flip. Air fry for an additional 5 minutes and recheck the internal temperature.

PER SERVING: Calories: 659; Total fat: 24g; Saturated fat: 8g; Cholesterol: 142mg; Sodium: 882mg; Carbohydrates: 56g; Fiber: 3g; Protein: 51g

Chicken Cordon Bleu

This beloved dish combines the flavors of chicken, ham, and Swiss cheese. Making it in the air fryer gives you a wonderfully crispy outside and an ooey-gooey inside bursting with rich flavor. Not to mention you can have it on the table within 35 minutes, which means you can make any night special in no time.

PREP TIME: 20 minutes
COOK TIME: 15 minutes
SERVES 4
TEMPERATURE: 360°F

2 boneless, skinless
  chicken breasts
Salt
Freshly ground black pepper
½ cup all-purpose flour
1 large egg
1 cup panko bread crumbs
¼ cup grated
  Parmesan cheese
1 teaspoon herbes de
  Provence
4 slices Swiss cheese
4 slices deli ham
Extra-virgin olive oil, for
  spraying

1. Cut the chicken breasts in half lengthwise so you have 4 very thin chicken breasts. Season with salt and pepper.

2. Put the flour in a small shallow bowl.

3. In a second small shallow bowl, beat the egg.

4. In a third small shallow bowl, combine the bread crumbs, Parmesan cheese, and herbes de Provence.

5. Preheat the air fryer to 360°F.

6. Place a slice each of Swiss cheese and ham on each chicken breast. Roll up the chicken and secure it with a couple of toothpicks.

7. Coat each rolled chicken breast with flour, then in the beaten egg, allowing any excess to drip off. Coat the chicken in the breading.

8. Lightly spray the air fryer basket with oil. Place the chicken in a single layer in the basket. (Air fry in batches, if necessary.) Lightly spray with oil.

9. Air fry for 10 minutes. Check the chicken to see if it has reached an internal temperature of 165°F. If it has, remove it from the air fryer. If it has not, air fry for 2 to 3 additional minutes, or until it has reached an internal temperature of 165°F.

PER SERVING: Calories: 357; Total fat: 13g; Saturated fat: 6g; Cholesterol: 124mg; Sodium: 597mg; Carbohydrates: 30g; Fiber: 1g; Protein: 30g

Chicken Tikka Skewers

Tikka has its roots in India and generally refers to meat that is marinated in yogurt and spices and then grilled. This recipe allows you to make it at home in the air fryer! Allow enough prep time for the chicken to marinate for the full 4 hours. It will really soak up the spices and flavors in the marinade.

GLUTEN-FREE

PREP TIME: 15 minutes, plus 4 hours to marinate

COOK TIME: 10 minutes

SERVES 4

TEMPERATURE: 400°F

1 cup plain yogurt

2 teaspoons minced garlic

2 teaspoons grated fresh ginger

1 teaspoon sweet chili sauce

1 teaspoon salt

½ teaspoon ground cumin

½ teaspoon turmeric

½ teaspoon cayenne pepper

½ teaspoon freshly ground black pepper

3 boneless, skinless chicken breasts, cut into 1-inch chunks

Extra-virgin olive oil, for spraying

1 lime, cut into wedges, for serving (optional)

1. In a large bowl, combine the yogurt, garlic, ginger, chili sauce, salt, cumin, turmeric, cayenne pepper, and black pepper.

2. Add the chicken and stir to coat. Cover the bowl and refrigerate for 4 hours or up to overnight.

3. Remove the chicken from the marinade and thread onto 6-inch metal skewers.

4. Preheat the air fryer to 400°F.

5. Lightly spray the air fryer basket with oil. Place the chicken skewers in a single layer in the basket. (Air fry in batches, if necessary.) Lightly spray with oil.

6. Air fry for 5 minutes. Flip the skewers and lightly spray with oil. Air fry for 5 additional minutes, or until the chicken is browned and has reached an internal temperature of 165°F.

7. Serve with lime wedges for squeezing over the chicken, if desired.

Variation: Feel free to add vegetables to the skewers between the pieces of chicken. Bump up the heat to this dish by increasing the amount of cayenne pepper added to the yogurt mixture.

PER SERVING: Calories: 147; Total fat: 5g; Saturated fat: 2g; Cholesterol: 68mg; Sodium: 668mg; Carbohydrates: 5g; Fiber: <1g; Protein: 21g

Roasted Turkey Legs

Roasted turkey legs are a great way to mix up your evening meals, and they are extremely quick and easy to make in the air fryer. Once you try this juicy and flavorful lean meat, you'll be hooked. Serve with anything from anything from Parmesan Roasted Zucchini (page 197) to Veggie-Stuffed Peppers (page 199).

DAIRY-FREE, GLUTEN-FREE, 30 MINUTES OR LESS

PREP TIME: 5 minutes
COOK TIME: 20 minutes
SERVES 4
TEMPERATURE: 380°F

4 turkey drumsticks
1½ teaspoons salt
1 teaspoon freshly ground black pepper
1 teaspoon smoked paprika
Extra-virgin olive oil, for spraying

1. Preheat the air fryer to 380°F.

2. Pat the turkey legs dry with paper towels.

3. In a small bowl, combine the salt, pepper, and paprika.

4. Rub the spice mixture on the turkey drumsticks, making sure to cover them completely.

5. Generously spray the air fryer basket with oil. Place the turkey legs in a single layer in the basket. (Air fry in batches, if necessary.) Generously spray with oil.

6. Air fry for 10 minutes. Flip the turkey legs and lightly spray with oil.

7. Air fry for an additional 5 minutes. Check the internal temperature. If it is over 165°F, remove the turkey from the air fryer basket. If the temperature has not reached 165°F, lightly spray the turkey with oil and flip again. Air fry for an additional 5 minutes, or until they reach 165°F.

Air Frying Tip: When you are air frying meat and trying to reach the correct internal temperature, be sure to check it every few minutes if you are adding extra cook time. The internal temperature can increase quickly, so you must be careful not to overcook the meat.

PER SERVING: Calories: 505; Total fat: 24g; Saturated fat: 7g; Cholesterol: 292mg; Sodium: 1,191mg; Carbohydrates: 1g; Fiber: <1g; Protein: 71g

Prosciutto and Spinach-Stuffed Turkey Breast

Change up your holiday dinners by serving this elegant stuffed turkey breast. It is easy to make for a weeknight dinner but sophisticated enough to serve guests. You will love how well it roasts in the air fryer, complemented with the bold flavors of the feta, Parmesan, and spinach stuffed inside.

GLUTEN-FREE

PREP TIME: 15 minutes
COOK TIME: 25 minutes, plus 10 minutes to rest
SERVES 4
TEMPERATURE: 370°F

1 (1½-pound) boneless turkey breast tenderloin
5 ounces frozen spinach, thawed and squeezed dry
½ cup crumbled feta cheese
¼ cup grated Parmesan cheese
2 teaspoons dried minced onion
3 pieces thinly sliced prosciutto
Salt
Freshly ground black pepper
Extra-virgin olive oil, for spraying

1. Butterfly the turkey breast and use a meat mallet to pound it to a ½-inch thickness.

2. In a small bowl, combine the spinach, feta cheese, Parmesan cheese, and dried onion.

3. Lay the prosciutto slices on the flattened turkey breast. Leaving ½ inch around the edges, top the prosciutto with the spinach mixture. Roll up the turkey and secure it with kitchen twine or toothpicks.

4. Preheat the air fryer to 370°F.

5. Season the rolled turkey with salt and pepper.

6. Generously spray the air fryer basket with oil. Place the turkey breast in the basket. Lightly spray with oil.

7. Air fry for 10 minutes. Carefully flip the turkey and lightly spray with oil. Air fry for an additional 10 to 15 minutes, or until it has reached an internal temperature of 165°F.

8. Let the turkey rest for 5 to 10 minutes before slicing and serving.

PER SERVING: Calories: 253; Total fat: 8g; Saturated fat: 4g; Cholesterol: 79mg; Sodium: 1,116mg; Carbohydrates: 9g; Fiber: 1g; Protein: 37g

Maple-Glazed Duck Breast

These duck breasts are a main course fit for a king or a queen, so surprise your favorite person with this for a special dinner at home or for date night. The glaze is sweet and savory with a hint of spice from the mustard and cayenne.

DAIRY-FREE, GLUTEN-FREE

PREP TIME: 5 minutes
COOK TIME: 25 minutes, plus 10 minutes to rest
SERVES 2
TEMPERATURE: 370°F

2 skin-on duck breasts
Salt
Freshly ground black pepper
2 tablespoons maple syrup
2 teaspoons Dijon mustard
1 teaspoon brown sugar
½ teaspoon cayenne pepper
Extra-virgin olive oil, for spraying

1. Preheat the air fryer to 370°F.

2. Score the duck breasts and season with salt and black pepper.

3. In a small bowl, whisk together the maple syrup, mustard, brown sugar, and cayenne pepper until well combined.

4. Lightly spray the air fryer basket with oil. Place the duck breasts skin-side down in the basket. Using a pastry brush, baste the tops with the glaze.

5. Air fry for 10 minutes. Carefully flip the duck breasts so the skin side is up and brush it with glaze. Air fry for an additional 10 to 15 minutes, or until the duck has reached an internal temperature of 165°F.

6. Let the duck rest for 5 to 10 minutes before slicing and serving.

PER SERVING: Calories: 546; Total fat: 24g; Saturated fat: 7g; Cholesterol: 178mg; Sodium: 274mg; Carbohydrates: 15g; Fiber: <1g; Protein: 63g

CHAPTER 6

Meat

Boneless Pork Chops

Boneless pork chops are a mainstay in many dinner repertoires because they are delicious as well as an excellent source of lean protein. They also cook up perfectly in the air fryer. For this version, I've used a classic seasoning combination of garlic, parsley, and thyme to help bring out the natural flavors of the pork.

DAIRY-FREE, GLUTEN-FREE, 30 MINUTES OR LESS

PREP TIME: 10 minutes
COOK TIME: 10 minutes, plus 5 minutes to rest
SERVES 4
TEMPERATURE: 370°F

1 teaspoon garlic powder
1 teaspoon dried
   garlic flakes
1 teaspoon dried parsley
½ teaspoon dried rosemary
½ teaspoon dried thyme
Salt
Freshly ground black pepper
4 (½-inch-thick) boneless
   pork chops
1 tablespoon extra-virgin
   olive oil, plus more for
   spraying

1. Preheat the air fryer to 370°F.

2. In a small bowl, combine the garlic powder, garlic flakes, parsley, rosemary, thyme, salt, and pepper.

3. Rub both sides of the pork chops with the olive oil, then coat each side with the garlic-herb mixture.

4. Lightly spray the air fryer basket with oil. Place the coated pork chops in a single layer in the basket, leaving ¼ inch between each to ensure even cooking.

5. Air fry for 4 to 5 minutes. Flip the pork chops and cook for an additional 4 to 5 minutes, or until they reach an internal temperature of at least 145°F.

6. Let the pork chops rest for 5 minutes before cutting. Serve warm.

Air Frying Tip: Using an air fryer rack for this recipe allows you to air-fry a larger quantity of pork chops without cooking in batches.

PER SERVING: Calories: 196; Total fat: 9g; Saturated fat: 3g; Cholesterol: 85mg; Sodium: 77mg; Carbohydrates: 1g; Fiber: <1g; Protein: 23g

Chicken Fried Steak

This classic American dish is typically panfried in oil. Using the air fryer results in a crispy steak without the heaviness. Serve with a side salad, mashed potatoes, or rice for a delicious complete meal.

30 MINUTES OR LESS

PREP TIME: 15 minutes
COOK TIME: 10 minutes
SERVES 4
TEMPERATURE: 400°F

4 beef cube steaks
Salt
Freshly ground black pepper
1 cup all-purpose flour
½ teaspoon garlic powder
½ teaspoon onion powder
½ teaspoon smoked paprika
¼ teaspoon cayenne pepper
1 large egg
½ cup buttermilk
Extra-virgin olive oil, for
    the basket

1. Preheat the air fryer to 400°F.

2. Season the beef generously with salt and black pepper.

3. In a small shallow bowl, mix together the flour, garlic powder, onion powder, smoked paprika, cayenne pepper, and a pinch of salt.

4. In a second small shallow bowl, combine the egg, buttermilk, and a pinch of salt. Whisk until smooth.

5. Coat each beef cube steak in the flour mixture, then in the buttermilk mixture, then in the flour mixture again.

6. Lightly spray the air fryer basket with oil. Place the coated cube steaks in a single layer in the basket, leaving ¼ inch between each to ensure even cooking.

7. Air fry for 4 to 5 minutes. Flip the steaks and air fry for an additional 4 to 5 minutes, or until they have reached an internal temperature of 145°F.

Variation: To make this recipe gluten-free, use a gluten-free flour, such as almond.

PER SERVING: Calories: 387; Total fat: 13g; Saturated fat: 5g; Cholesterol: 152mg; Sodium: 96mg; Carbohydrates: 26g; Fiber: 1g; Protein: 41g

Jerk-Flavored Pork Loin Roast

A pork loin roast is a tender cut of meat that tends to be lean. The bold flavors of jerk seasoning combine the traditional taste of the Caribbean with sweet and smoky seasonings for a memorable meal.

DAIRY-FREE, GLUTEN-FREE

PREP TIME: 10 minutes, plus 4 hours to marinate and 20 minutes to reach room temperature

COOK TIME: 20 minutes
SERVES 4
TEMPERATURE: 390°F

2 tablespoons extra-virgin olive oil, plus more for the basket

2 tablespoons light brown sugar

2 teaspoons allspice

1 teaspoon salt

½ teaspoon ground cumin

½ teaspoon freshly ground black pepper

½ teaspoon cayenne pepper

½ teaspoon red pepper flakes

¼ teaspoon ground cloves

¼ teaspoon ground cinnamon

1½ pounds pork loin roast, trimmed of fat

1. Preheat the air fryer to 390°F.

2. In a small bowl, combine the extra-virgin olive oil, brown sugar, allspice, salt, cumin, black pepper, cayenne pepper, red pepper flakes, cloves, and cinnamon. Stir to create a thick paste.

3. Cut the pork loin roast into large pieces that are no thicker than ½ inch.

4. Rub the jerk seasoning paste into the pork pieces, coating on all sides. Transfer the coated pork to a container. Cover and refrigerate for at least 4 hours and up to overnight.

5. Let the pork sit on the counter for 20 minutes to come to room temperature.

6. Preheat the air fryer to 390°F.

7. Lightly spray the air fryer basket with oil. Place the pork in a single layer in the basket, leaving ¼ inch between each piece to ensure even cooking.

8. Air fry for 10 minutes. Flip the pork and air fry for an additional 10 minutes, or until it has reached an internal temperature of at least 145°F.

Air Frying Tip: For the best results and even cooking, keep meats about ½ inch thick.

PER SERVING: Calories: 307; Total fat: 14g; Saturated fat: 3g; Cholesterol: 107mg; Sodium: 675mg; Carbohydrates: 6g; Fiber: 1g; Protein: 38g

Honey Mustard-Glazed Ham

Glazed ham is always a holiday crowd-pleaser. This simple honey-mustard version is perfect for everyday eating or special events, and pairs wonderfully with any potatoes or vegetable sides you usually serve.

DAIRY-FREE, GLUTEN-FREE

PREP TIME: 5 minutes
COOK TIME: 45 minutes
SERVES 6
TEMPERATURE: 390°F

1 (3-pound) fully cooked
   boneless ham
¼ cup packed light
   brown sugar
2 tablespoons honey
1 tablespoon Dijon mustard
½ tablespoon
   pineapple juice

1. Preheat the air fryer to 390°F.

2. Remove the ham from the package and wrap it in a large piece of aluminum foil.

3. Place the foil-wrapped ham in the air fryer basket. Air fry for 30 minutes.

4. While the ham is cooking, in a small bowl, combine the brown sugar, honey, mustard, and pineapple juice. Whisk until well combined.

5. Remove the foil from the ham and glaze the ham all over. Air fry for an additional 15 minutes, reglazing every 5 minutes.

6. Slice and serve.

Air Frying Tip: Covering food with foil in the air fryer will prevent it from burning or becoming too crispy on the outside while cooking.

PER SERVING: Calories: 424; Total fat: 24g; Saturated fat: 8g; Cholesterol: 1,22mg; Sodium: 2,614mg; Carbohydrates: 19g; Fiber: <1g; Protein: 37g

Baked Sausage and Peppers

A delightful dinner made with the air fryer doesn't have to be complicated. This recipe requires only a few ingredients, and in 30 minutes you'll have a delicious, well-balanced meal on the table. Serve with dinner rolls or buns to round out the meal.

DAIRY-FREE, 30 MINUTES OR LESS

PREP TIME: 10 minutes
COOK TIME: 20 minutes
SERVES 4
TEMPERATURE: 375°F

4 bell peppers (red, yellow, or orange)
Extra-virgin olive oil, for spraying
Salt
Freshly ground black pepper
4 precooked smoked sausages

1. Preheat the air fryer to 375°F.

2. Remove the bell pepper stems and seeds and cut into ½-inch-thick strips.

3. Lightly spray the air fryer basket with oil. Place the pepper strips in the basket. Lightly spray with oil and season with salt and pepper to taste.

4. Air fry for 7 to 10 minutes, or until the peppers start to get tender.

5. Cut a small slit in the smoked sausages and add them to the air fryer. Air fry for an additional 5 to 10 minutes, or until the sausages are warmed through and the peppers are nicely roasted and slightly charred.

Air Frying Tip: Cook times for vegetables will vary based on the size of the vegetable pieces and your preferences. Some people prefer their vegetables only barely cooked and still crunchy. Cook the veggies longer for a tender result. For charred vegetables, keep cooking and add additional olive oil.

PER SERVING: Calories: 242; Total fat: 15g; Saturated fat: 5g; Cholesterol: 52mg; Sodium: 709mg; Carbohydrates: 16g; Fiber: 4g; Protein: 11g

Mongolian Beef

Flank steak is a must for this classic recipe that requires no takeout box. The results are tender, flavorful strips of beef that pair well with steamed broccoli and rice for a delicious and healthy dinner.

DAIRY-FREE

PREP TIME: 10 minutes, plus 1 hour to marinate
COOK TIME: 15 minutes
SERVES 4
TEMPERATURE: 400°F

¼ cup soy sauce
1 tablespoon hoisin sauce
1 tablespoon sesame oil
1 tablespoon minced garlic
2 teaspoons granulated sugar
1 teaspoon red pepper flakes
1 pound beef flank steak, thinly sliced
Extra-virgin olive oil, for greasing the basket

1. In a small bowl, whisk together the soy sauce, hoisin sauce, sesame oil, garlic, sugar, and red pepper flakes.

2. Toss the sliced flank steak with the marinade, cover, and refrigerate for at least 1 hour and up to overnight.

3. Preheat the air fryer to 400°F.

4. Lightly spray the air fryer basket with oil. Place the steak in the basket.

5. Air fry for 12 to 15 minutes, or until the steak is no longer pink and is starting to brown.

Air Frying Tip: Cutting the steak into equal-size slices will ensure even cooking. Always make sure the beef reaches an internal temperature of 145°F.

PER SERVING: Calories: 259; Total fat: 14g; Saturated fat: 5g; Cholesterol: 55mg; Sodium: 1,010mg; Carbohydrates: 5g; Fiber: <1g; Protein: 25g

Mozzarella-Stuffed Beef Meatballs

Finding fresh mozzarella cheese inside a meatball is a fun surprise. These meatballs will be gone in minutes. Serve alongside mashed potatoes for a homestyle dinner or with Spicy Italian Zucchini Boats (page 188) for a twist.

30 MINUTES OR LESS

PREP TIME: 15 minutes
COOK TIME: 15 minutes
SERVES 4
TEMPERATURE: 390°F

1 pound lean ground beef
½ cup panko bread crumbs
1 large egg, beaten
2 teaspoons dried parsley
1 teaspoon minced garlic
½ teaspoon salt
½ teaspoon freshly ground
   black pepper
20 fresh mini
   mozzarella pearls
Extra-virgin olive oil, for
   the basket
Marinara sauce, for serving
   (optional)

1. Preheat the air fryer to 390°F.

2. In a large bowl, combine the ground beef, bread crumbs, egg, parsley, garlic, salt, and pepper.

3. Using a 1-inch cookie scoop, shape the mixture into meatballs. You should have about 20 meatballs.

4. Press one mozzarella cheese pearl into the center of each meatball, making sure the meat completely covers the cheese.

5. Lightly spray the air fryer basket with oil. Place the meatballs in the basket.

6. Air fry for 6 minutes, then shake the basket to reposition the meatballs to ensure even cooking. Air fry for an additional 4 to 9 minutes, or until the meat is browned and crispy and has reached an internal temperature of 160°F.

7. Serve with marinara sauce, if using.

Air Frying Tip: The cook time can vary based on the size of your meatballs.

PER SERVING: Calories: 315; Total fat: 15g; Saturated fat: 6g; Cholesterol: 151mg; Sodium: 410mg; Carbohydrates: 8g; Fiber: <1g; Protein: 34g

Classic Hamburgers

Hamburgers are an American classic and a perennial favorite. Making burgers in the air fryer is easy, and I love that the crisper plate allows the excess grease to drip away. These burgers turn out tender and juicy inside and nice and crispy on the outside—just the way you want them.

PREP TIME: 10 minutes
COOK TIME: 20 minutes
SERVES 4
TEMPERATURE: 370°F

1 pound ground beef
1 teaspoon salt
½ teaspoon freshly ground
   black pepper
½ teaspoon garlic powder
Extra-virgin olive oil, for
   the basket
4 slices cheese (optional)
4 hamburger buns
Lettuce, pickles, onions,
   or tomatoes, for topping
   (optional)

1. Preheat the air fryer to 370°F.

2. Season the beef with the salt, pepper, and garlic powder, then form into 4 equal-size patties.

3. Spray the air fryer basket lightly with oil. Place the burgers in a single layer in the basket.

4. Air fry for 8 minutes. Flip the burgers and air fry for an additional 7 to 9 minutes. Add a slice of cheese to each patty, if using, and air fry for about 30 seconds, or until the cheese melts.

5. Assemble the burgers on the buns with any desired toppings.

Air Frying Tip: According to the USDA, the minimum safe temperature for ground meat is 160°F, or well-done. The cook times in this recipe are for a well-done burger. If you prefer your burger rare, it will take about 10 total minutes and should reach 125°F. If you prefer a medium-rare burger, it will take about 12 total minutes and should reach 135°F. If you like a medium burger, it will take about 14 total minutes and should reach 155°F.

PER SERVING: Calories: 410; Total fat: 20g; Saturated fat: 7g; Cholesterol: 100mg; Sodium: 878mg; Carbohydrates: 22g; Fiber: 1g; Protein: 33g

Baby Back Ribs

Cooking Baby Back Ribs in the air fryer may sound unusual, but the results will surprise you. Tender, juicy ribs with a crispy surface texture will have you asking for seconds. Use your favorite barbecue sauce and serve with a simple coleslaw for a fun meal.

DAIRY-FREE

PREP TIME: 5 minutes
COOK TIME: 40 minutes
SERVES 4
TEMPERATURE: 400°F

1 rack of baby back ribs, cut into 3 or 4 sections
1 teaspoon smoked paprika
1 teaspoon chili powder
1 teaspoon onion powder
1 teaspoon garlic powder
1 teaspoon light brown sugar
1 teaspoon salt
1 teaspoon freshly ground black pepper
Extra-virgin olive oil, for the basket
1 cup barbecue sauce

1. Preheat the air fryer to 400°F.

2. Remove the membrane from the back of the ribs.

3. In a small bowl, combine the paprika, chili powder, onion powder, garlic powder, brown sugar, salt, and pepper.

4. Season the ribs on both sides with the seasoning mixture.

5. Lightly spray the air fryer basket with oil. Place the ribs meat-side down in a single layer in the basket. (Air fry in batches, if necessary.)

6. Air fry for 20 minutes. Flip the ribs and air fry for an additional 15 to 20 minutes, depending on the thickness.

7. Using a pastry brush, brush the barbecue sauce over the ribs, then air fry for 5 minutes.

Air Frying Tip: According to the USDA, the minimum safe temperature for pork is 145°F. Remember, cook time will vary based on the thickness of the ribs. Always use a meat thermometer to determine whether the meat is cooked to the correct internal temperature.

PER SERVING: Calories: 742; Total fat: 43g; Saturated fat: 16g; Cholesterol: 195mg; Sodium: 1,460mg; Carbohydrates: 31g; Fiber: 1g; Protein: 53g

Pork Schnitzel

Schnitzel is a dish that was made famous by the Austrians but dates back to the ancient world. It is essentially a thin slice of breaded and fried meat. Air fried Pork Schnitzel has less fat because it's not fried in large amounts of oil, and it creates the perfect balance of crispy on the outside, yet tender and juicy on the inside. It's perfect for a family dinner with mashed potatoes and a salad.

30 MINUTES OR LESS

PREP TIME: 15 minutes
COOK TIME: 15 minutes
SERVES 4
TEMPERATURE: 370°F

4 boneless pork chops
½ cup all-purpose flour
1 teaspoon salt, divided
1 teaspoon freshly ground
  black pepper, divided
1 large egg
1 cup panko bread crumbs
¼ teaspoon garlic powder
¼ teaspoon Old Bay
  seasoning
¼ teaspoon dried sage
Extra-virgin olive oil, for
  spraying

1. Pat the pork chops dry with a paper towel. Lay the pork chops between two pieces of plastic wrap. Using a meat mallet or a rolling pin, pound the chops to ¼-inch-thick cutlets.

2. Preheat the air fryer to 370°F.

3. In a small shallow bowl, combine the flour, ½ teaspoon salt, and ½ teaspoon pepper.

4. In a second small shallow bowl, beat the egg.

5. In a third small shallow bowl, combine the bread crumbs, garlic powder, Old Bay, dried sage, remaining ½ teaspoon salt, and remaining ½ teaspoon pepper.

6. Coat the pork chops in the flour mixture, then in the beaten egg, then in the breading until fully coated.

7. Lightly spray the air fryer basket with oil. Place the coated pork chops in a single layer in the basket. Lightly spray with oil.

8. Air fry for 8 minutes. Flip the pork chops and air fry for an additional 6 to 8 minutes, or until the pork is golden brown and crispy and has reached an internal temperature of 145°F.

PER SERVING: Calories: 277; Total fat: 6g; Saturated fat: 2g; Cholesterol: 96mg; Sodium: 886mg; Carbohydrates: 28g; Fiber: 1g; Protein: 28g

Peppered Rib Eye Steak

Freshly ground black pepper really makes a rib eye steak shine. I love using my air fryer as an indoor "grilling" option when the weather is not good for outdoor cooking. Serve these steaks with Onion Rings (page 79) for a real treat!

DAIRY-FREE, GLUTEN-FREE, 30 MINUTES OR LESS

PREP TIME: 5 minutes
COOK TIME: 15 minutes, plus 5 minutes to rest
SERVES 4
TEMPERATURE: 400°F

1 teaspoon salt
1 teaspoon freshly ground black pepper
¾ teaspoon garlic powder
¾ teaspoon paprika
½ teaspoon dried thyme
½ teaspoon dried oregano
¼ teaspoon cayenne pepper
¼ teaspoon red pepper flakes
4 (8-ounce) rib eye steaks (1½ inches thick)
Extra-virgin olive oil, for the basket

1. Preheat the air fryer to 400°F.

2. In a small bowl, combine the salt, black pepper, garlic powder, paprika, thyme, oregano, cayenne pepper, and red pepper flakes.

3. Sprinkle the seasoning mixture on both sides of the steaks, pressing it into the sides with your fingers to ensure it adheres.

4. Lightly spray the air fryer basket with oil. Place the steaks in a single layer in the basket. Do not overcrowd. (Air fry in batches, if necessary.)

5. Air fry for 6 minutes. Flip the steaks and air fry for an additional 6 minutes for a medium steak.

6. Let the steaks rest for 5 minutes. Slice against the grain and serve.

Air Frying Tip: The cook times for different levels of doneness are as follows: rare (internal temperature of 125°F) will cook approximately 9 minutes; medium-rare (internal temperature of 135°F) will cook for approximately 10 minutes; medium-well (internal temperature of 150°F to 155°F) will cook for approximately 13 minutes; well-done (internal temperature of 160°F+) will cook for approximately 15 minutes. It is especially important to watch your steaks closely during the end of the cook time so they will be cooked to your preference. Cook times with each air fryer model will vary, so check the meat frequently while cooking.

PER SERVING: Calories: 593; Total fat: 47g; Saturated fat: 18g; Cholesterol: 172mg; Sodium: 702mg; Carbohydrates: 1g; Fiber: 1g; Protein: 43g

Ranch-Bacon-Cheddar Sliders

The first time I made these delightful little sliders I knew the recipe was going to be a hit. My children have been asking for them ever since! Serve with Classic French Fries (page 191), Creole Carrot Fries (page 176), or a simple green salad.

30 MINUTES OR LESS

PREP TIME: 10 minutes
COOK TIME: 15 minutes
SERVES 4
TEMPERATURE: 370°F

1 pound ground beef
2 tablespoons dry ranch
   dressing mix
½ cup crumbled
   cooked bacon
1 cup shredded
   cheddar cheese
Extra-virgin olive oil, for
   the basket
1 package slider buns
Lettuce, pickles, onions,
   or tomatoes, for topping
   (optional)

1. Preheat the air fryer to 370°F.

2. In a medium bowl, combine the ground beef, ranch dressing mix, crumbled bacon, and cheddar cheese.

3. Form the meat mixture into 8 small slider-size patties.

4. Lightly spray the air fryer basket with oil. Place the sliders in a single layer in the basket, leaving ¼ inch between each to ensure even cooking. (Air fry in batches, if necessary.)

5. Air fry for 6 minutes. Flip the sliders and air fry for an additional 4 to 9 minutes, or until cooked to your desired level of doneness (see Tip).

6. Assemble the sliders on the buns with any desired toppings.

Air Frying Tip: According to the USDA, the minimum safe temperature for ground meat is 160°F, or well-done. The cook times in this recipe are for a well-done burger. If you prefer your burger rare, it will take about 10 total minutes and should reach 125°F. If you prefer a medium-rare burger, it will take about 12 total minutes and should reach 135°F. If you like a medium burger, it will take about 14 total minutes and should reach 155°F.

PER SERVING: Calories: 764; Total fat: 37g; Saturated fat: 14g; Cholesterol: 138mg; Sodium: 864mg; Carbohydrates: 64g; Fiber: 3g; Protein: 51g

Mustard-Herb Sirloin Steak

A sirloin steak is a budget-friendly option that does not sacrifice on flavor. Serve with Classic French Fries (page 191) or Baby Potatoes (page 186) for a dinner everyone will request again and again.

DAIRY-FREE, GLUTEN-FREE, 30 MINUTES OR LESS

PREP TIME: 5 minutes, plus 30 minutes to reach room temperature

COOK TIME: 10 minutes, plus 5 minutes to rest

SERVES 4

TEMPERATURE: 400°F

2 sirloin steaks
   (1½ inches thick)
2 tablespoons Dijon mustard
2 teaspoons Italian
   seasoning
½ teaspoon garlic powder
Salt
Freshly ground black pepper
Extra-virgin olive oil, for
   greasing the basket

1. Allow the steaks to sit out on the counter for 30 minutes, or until they reach room temperature.

2. Preheat the air fryer to 400°F.

3. In a small bowl, combine the mustard, Italian seasoning, and garlic powder.

4. Season the steaks all over with salt and pepper.

5. Lightly spray the air fryer basket with oil. Place the steaks in a single layer in the basket. Do not overcrowd. (Air fry in batches, if necessary.) If the steaks are too big for the basket, you can cut them into 2 or 3 large sections.

6. Air fry for 6 minutes. Flip the steaks and air fry for an additional 6 minutes for a medium steak.

7. Let the steaks rest for 5 minutes before slicing and serving.

Air Frying Tip: The cook times for different levels of doneness are as follows: rare (internal temperature of 125°F) will cook approximately 9 minutes; medium-rare (internal temperature of 135°F) will cook for approximately 10 minutes; medium-well (internal temperature of 150°F to 155°F) will cook for approximately 13 minutes; well-done (internal temperature of 160°F+) will cook for approximately 15 minutes. It is especially important to watch your steaks closely during the end of the cook time so they will be cooked to your preference.

PER SERVING: Calories: 124; Total fat: 8g; Saturated fat: 3g; Cholesterol: 42mg; Sodium: 210mg; Carbohydrates: 1g; Fiber: 1g; Protein: 12g

Lemon-Dijon Lamb Chops

Lamb loin chops are taken from the waist of the animal and do not contain any rib bones. It is a very tender cut of meat. The marinade enhances the flavor of the lamb and results in a delectable main dish.

DAIRY-FREE, GLUTEN-FREE, 30 MINUTES OR LESS

PREP TIME: 5 minutes
COOK TIME: 12 minutes, plus 5 minutes to rest
SERVES 4
TEMPERATURE: 380°F

2 tablespoons Dijon mustard
1 tablespoon freshly squeezed lemon juice
1 teaspoon dried basil
1 teaspoon salt
½ teaspoon freshly ground black pepper
4 loin lamb chops
Extra-virgin olive oil, for greasing the basket

1. Preheat the air fryer to 380°F.

2. In a small bowl, combine the mustard, lemon juice, basil, salt, and pepper.

3. Pat the lamb chops dry with a paper towel.

4. Using a pastry brush, coat the lamb chops all over with the mustard sauce.

5. Lightly spray the air fryer basket with oil. Place the coated lamb chops in in a single layer in the basket. Do not overcrowd. (Air fry in batches, if necessary.)

6. Air fry for 6 minutes. Flip the chops and air fry for an additional 6 minutes for medium lamb chops.

7. Let the lamb chops rest for 5 minutes before serving.

Air Frying Tip: Cook times with each air fryer model will vary, so check the meat frequently while cooking to reach your preferred level of doneness.

PER SERVING: Calories: 329; Total fat: 27g; Saturated fat: 11g; Cholesterol: 80mg; Sodium: 834mg; Carbohydrates: 1g; Fiber: <1g; Protein: 19g

Spice-Rubbed T-Bone Steak

The satisfying flavor of a T-bone steak is unmatched. The rub I've created is full of savory flavors that will please your taste buds and accentuate the meat perfectly. Pair with Baby Potatoes (page 186) for a delicious dinner.

DAIRY-FREE, GLUTEN-FREE

PREP TIME: 5 minutes, plus 30 minutes to reach room temperature

COOK TIME: 10 minutes, plus 5 minutes to rest

SERVES 4

TEMPERATURE: 400°F

2 T-bone steaks

1 teaspoon smoked paprika

1 teaspoon salt

1 teaspoon freshly ground black pepper

¼ teaspoon onion powder

¼ teaspoon garlic powder

¼ teaspoon cayenne pepper

¼ teaspoon ground coriander

⅛ teaspoon ground turmeric

1 tablespoon extra-virgin olive oil, plus more for the basket

1. Allow the steaks to sit on the counter for 30 minutes, or until they reach room temperature.

2. Preheat the air fryer to 400°F.

3. In a small bowl, combine the paprika, salt, black pepper, onion powder, garlic powder, cayenne pepper, coriander, and turmeric.

4. Rub the olive oil over both sides of the steaks. Season with the seasoning mix.

5. Lightly spray the air fryer basket with oil. Place the steaks in a single layer in the basket. Do not overcrowd. (Air fry in batches, if necessary.)

6. Air fry for 6 minutes. Flip the steaks and air fry for an additional 6 minutes for a medium steak.

7. Let the steaks rest for 5 minutes before slicing and serving.

Air Frying Tip: The cook times for different levels of doneness are as follows: rare (internal temperature of 125°F) will cook approximately 9 minutes; medium-rare (internal temperature of 135°F) will cook for approximately 10 minutes; medium-well (internal temperature of 150°F to 155°F) will cook for approximately 13 minutes; well-done (internal temperature of 160°F+) will cook for approximately 15 minutes. It is especially important to watch your steaks closely during the end of the cook time so they will be cooked to your preference.

PER SERVING: Calories: 164; Total fat: 12g; Saturated fat: 4g; Cholesterol: 35mg; Sodium: 610mg; Carbohydrates: 1g; Fiber: 1g; Protein: 12g

Garlic and Herb Rack of Lamb

Rack of lamb is an elegant meal that is usually served on holidays or special occasions or when entertaining. But with the air fryer, it's so easy to make that you can whip it up any night of the week. Most racks of lamb contain 7 or 8 ribs sections and serve 4 people. Serve with Baby Potatoes (page 186) or herbed rice.

DAIRY-FREE, GLUTEN-FREE

PREP TIME: 10 minutes

COOK TIME: 10 minutes, plus 10 minutes to rest

SERVES 4

TEMPERATURE: 380°F

1 (1½- to 2-pound) rack of lamb, frenched

1 tablespoon extra-virgin olive oil, plus more for the basket

1 tablespoon finely chopped fresh parsley

½ tablespoon finely chopped fresh thyme

½ tablespoon finely chopped fresh rosemary

1 tablespoon minced garlic

1 teaspoon salt

½ teaspoon freshly ground black pepper

1. Cut the rack of lamb into two so it will fit in the air fryer basket.

2. Preheat the air fryer to 380°F.

3. In a small bowl, combine the olive oil, parsley, thyme, rosemary, garlic, salt, and pepper.

4. Rub the herb mixture all over the rack of lamb.

5. Lightly spray the air fryer basket with oil. Place the rack of lamb fat-side up in a single layer in the basket. Do not overcrowd. (Air fry in batches, if necessary.)

6. Air fry for 12 minutes, or until the lamb has reached an internal temperature of 145°F for medium.

7. Let the lamb rest for 7 minutes before serving.

Air Frying Tip: Cook times with each air fryer model will vary, so check the meat frequently while cooking to reach your preferred level of doneness.

PER SERVING: Calories: 321; Total fat: 20g; Saturated fat: 8g; Cholesterol: 105mg; Sodium: 696mg; Carbohydrates: 1g; Fiber: <1g; Protein: 34g

Breaded Veal Cutlets

Veal cutlets are boneless portions of meat from the leg of a calf. These thin, mild cuts of meat taste great breaded and fried.

DAIRY-FREE, 30 MINUTES OR LESS

PREP TIME: 15 minutes
COOK TIME: 15 minutes
SERVES 4
TEMPERATURE: 370°F

½ cup all-purpose flour
½ teaspoon salt
½ teaspoon freshly ground
   black pepper
2 large eggs
1½ cups panko
   bread crumbs
1 teaspoon garlic powder
1 teaspoon onion powder
Pinch cayenne pepper
4 veal cutlets
Extra-virgin olive oil, for
   the basket

1. In a small shallow bowl, combine the flour, salt, and black pepper.

2. In a second small shallow bowl, beat the eggs.

3. In a third small shallow bowl, combine the bread crumbs, garlic powder, onion powder, and cayenne pepper.

4. Coat the veal cutlets in the flour mixture, then in the beaten eggs. Let any excess egg drip off the meat. Coat the cutlets in the breading. Press on the breading gently to ensure it adheres.

5. Preheat the air fryer to 370°F.

6. Lightly spray the air fryer basket with oil. Place the coated veal cutlets in a single layer in the basket. Do not overcrowd. (Air fry in batches, if necessary.)

7. Air fry for 8 minutes. Flip the cutlets and air fry for an additional 6 minutes, or until the veal is lightly browned and crispy and has reached an internal temperature of 145°F.

Air Frying Tip: If you cannot find veal cutlets, you can buy veal chops and use a meat mallet to pound them to a ¼-inch thickness.

PER SERVING: Calories: 324; Total fat: 5g; Saturated fat: 2g; Cholesterol: 145mg; Sodium: 468mg; Carbohydrates: 36g; Fiber: 1g; Protein: 33g

Tuscan Pork Kebabs

For this Tuscan-inspired dish, pork and vegetables are coated in a fresh, rich, peppery herb-and-spice blend. These kebabs are loaded with lean and tender pork and fresh vegetables. They are wonderful to make in the summer, when gardens and farmers' markets are bursting with fresh vegetables.

DAIRY-FREE, GLUTEN-FREE, 30 MINUTES OR LESS

PREP TIME: 15 minutes
COOK TIME: 10 minutes
SERVES 4
TEMPERATURE: 370°F

1 pound pork tenderloin
½ teaspoon dried oregano
½ teaspoon dried basil
½ teaspoon dried thyme
½ teaspoon dried marjoram
½ teaspoon garlic powder
½ teaspoon salt
½ teaspoon freshly ground
   black pepper
¼ teaspoon dried rosemary
2 medium zucchini, sliced
2 medium yellow
   squash, sliced
2 red bell peppers, cut
   into chunks
1 red onion, cut into chunks
2 tablespoons extra-virgin
   olive oil, plus more for
   spraying

1. Cut the pork tenderloin into 1-inch cubes.

2. In a small bowl, combine the oregano, basil, thyme, marjoram, garlic powder, salt, and black pepper.

3. In a medium bowl, toss the pork, zucchini, squash, bell peppers, and onion with the olive oil and seasoning mixture to coat.

4. Preheat the air fryer to 370°F.

5. Thread the pork and vegetables in an alternating pattern onto 6-inch metal skewers.

6. Lightly spray the air fryer basket with oil. Place the skewers in a single layer in the basket. Lightly spray with oil.

7. Air fry for 5 minutes. Flip the skewers and lightly spray with oil. Air fry for an additional 4 to 5 minutes, or until the pork reaches an internal temperature of 145°F.

Air Frying Tip: Many air fryer accessory kits contain 6-inch metal skewers and a grilling rack for the skewers to sit on. They work great for all kinds of kebab recipes.

PER SERVING: Calories: 246; Total fat: 10g; Saturated fat: 2g; Cholesterol: 74mg; Sodium: 375mg; Carbohydrates: 13g; Fiber: 4g; Protein: 27g

Teriyaki-Ginger Steak Kebabs

The marinade on these beef kebabs is rich, sweet, and bold, and it caramelizes beautifully on the meat. Serve with white rice or steamed broccoli on the side.

DAIRY-FREE

PREP TIME: 25 minutes, plus 3 hours to marinate

COOK TIME: 20 minutes

SERVES 4

TEMPERATURE: 350°F

¾ cup teriyaki sauce

¼ cup pineapple juice

1 tablespoon soy sauce

1 tablespoon light brown sugar

1 tablespoon minced garlic

½ teaspoon red pepper flakes

½ tablespoon grated fresh ginger

1 pound beef sirloin steak, cut into 1-inch cubes

1 large sweet onion, cut into 1-inch cubes

2 bell peppers (red, yellow, or orange), cut into 1-inch chunks

1 small pineapple, peeled, cored, and cut into 1-inch chunks

Extra-virgin olive oil, for the basket

1. In a small saucepan over medium-high heat, combine the teriyaki sauce, pineapple juice, soy sauce, brown sugar, garlic, red pepper flakes, and ginger. Heat just until it comes to a boil, then reduce the heat to low and simmer for 5 minutes. Remove from the heat and let cool for 5 to 10 minutes.

2. Pour half of the marinade into a large zip-top bag. Reserve the rest to use during cooking.

3. Place the beef cubes in the zip-top bag and make sure the beef is well coated. Seal the bag and refrigerate for 3 hours to marinate.

4. Preheat the air fryer to 350°F.

5. Thread the beef, vegetables, and pineapple in an alternating pattern onto 6-inch metal skewers.

6. Lightly spray the air fryer basket with oil. Place the skewers in a single layer in the basket.

7. Air fry for 8 minutes. Flip the skewers and brush some of the reserved marinade onto the skewers with a pastry brush. Air fry for an additional 4 minutes, or until the beef reaches an internal temperature of 145°F.

PER SERVING: Calories: 369; Total fat: 6g; Saturated fat: 2g; Cholesterol: 58mg; Sodium: 2,375mg; Carbohydrates: 50g; Fiber: 5g; Protein: 33g

Parmesan-Crusted Pork Chops

Parmesan cheese and Cajun seasoning combine to make a crunchy, flavorful coating for these pork chops. Whether you're serving them to your family or to guests, this quick and easy dish is sure to be a hit.

GLUTEN-FREE, 30 MINUTES OR LESS

PREP TIME: 10 minutes
COOK TIME: 10 minutes, plus 3 minutes to rest
SERVES 4
TEMPERATURE: 400°F

1 large egg
1 cup shredded
   Parmesan cheese
1 teaspoon Cajun seasoning
4 bone-in pork chops
Extra-virgin olive oil, for
   spraying

1. Preheat the air fryer to 400°F.

2. In a small shallow bowl, beat the egg.

3. In a second small shallow bowl, combine the Parmesan cheese and Cajun seasoning.

4. Coat the pork chops in the beaten egg, then in the cheese mixture. Press on the cheese mixture to ensure it adheres.

5. Lightly spray the air fryer basket with oil. Place the coated pork chops in a single layer in the basket, leaving 1 inch between each to ensure even cooking. Lightly spray with oil.

6. Air fry for 5 minutes. Flip the chops and lightly spray with oil. Air fry for an additional 5 minutes, or until the pork has reached an internal temperature of 145°F.

7. Remove from the air fryer and let the pork rest for 3 minutes before serving.

PER SERVING: Calories: 292; Total fat: 17g; Saturated fat: 7g; Cholesterol: 133mg; Sodium: 415mg; Carbohydrates: 1g; Fiber: 0g; Protein: 32g

CHAPTER 7

Seafood

Teriyaki Shrimp Skewers

Teriyaki sauce complements juicy shrimp and fresh pineapple beautifully in this easy, flavorful recipe. These skewers are quick to make and taste great with a side of rice or noodles. Add some steamed broccoli for a complete meal.

DAIRY-FREE, 30 MINUTES OR LESS

PREP TIME: 10 minutes
COOK TIME: 10 minutes
SERVES 4
TEMPERATURE: 400°F

1 pound jumbo shrimp, peeled and deveined
½ cup teriyaki sauce
1 pineapple, peeled, cored, and cut into 1-inch chunks
Extra-virgin olive oil, for the basket

1. Preheat the air fryer to 400°F.

2. In a medium bowl, combine the shrimp and teriyaki sauce.

3. Thread the coated shrimp and pineapple chunks in an alternating pattern onto 6-inch metal skewers.

4. Lightly spray the air fryer basket with oil. Place the skewers in a single layer in the basket.

5. Air fry for 5 minutes. Flip the skewers and brush more teriyaki sauce onto the shrimp, if desired. Air fry for an additional 5 minutes.

Air Frying Tip: If you use wooden skewers in your air fryer, be sure to soak them in water for 30 minutes first to prevent them from charring or burning.

PER SERVING: Calories: 265; Total fat: 2g; Saturated fat: 0g; Cholesterol: 170mg; Sodium: 1,552mg; Carbohydrates: 35g; Fiber: 3g; Protein: 26g

Tropical Tuna Steaks

Pineapples, hoisin, ginger, and lime juice combine to make a delightfully tropical-tasting marinade for fresh ahi tuna steaks. You need only 5 minutes to cook this glorious dish in the air fryer, and it turns out perfect every time.

DAIRY-FREE, GLUTEN-FREE

PREP TIME: 10 minutes, plus 30 minutes to marinate

COOK TIME: 5 minutes, plus 5 minutes to rest

SERVES 4

TEMPERATURE: 380°F

½ cup crushed pineapple

¼ cup hoisin sauce

2 tablespoons freshly squeezed lime juice

1 tablespoon chopped cilantro

2 teaspoons honey

1 teaspoon minced fresh ginger

1 teaspoon minced garlic

1 teaspoon extra-virgin olive oil, plus more for spraying

½ teaspoon sriracha

4 (6-ounce) ahi tuna steaks

1. In a small bowl, combine the pineapple, hoisin sauce, lime juice, cilantro, honey, ginger, olive oil, and sriracha.

2. Place three-quarters of the marinade in a large zip-top bag and reserve the remaining marinade. Add the tuna steaks to the zip-top bag and coat them in the marinade. Seal the bag and refrigerate for 30 minutes.

3. Preheat the air fryer to 380°F.

4. Remove the tuna steaks from the marinade and shake off any excess.

5. Lightly spray the air fryer basket with oil. Place the tuna steaks in a single layer in the basket. Lightly spray with oil.

6. Air fry for 5 minutes. Brush the reserved marinade on the tuna steaks, then let them rest for 5 minutes before slicing and serving.

Air Frying Tip: Tuna is a very lean fish and does not reheat well using the air fryer or any other method. Eat immediately after cooking or use the leftovers in salads or other cold dishes that do not require reheating.

PER SERVING: Calories: 258; Total fat: 3g; Saturated fat: <1g; Cholesterol: 38mg; Sodium: 305mg; Carbohydrates: 16g; Fiber: 1g; Protein: 43g

Cajun Shrimp and Veggies

This recipe brings home the flavors of Louisiana for a quick and easy weeknight meal. The vegetables, shrimp, and smoked sausage are coated in a tasty Cajun seasoning and roasted to perfection. Pair with Easy Biscuits (page 221) for a hearty meal.

DAIRY-FREE, GLUTEN-FREE,
30 MINUTES OR LESS

PREP TIME: 10 minutes
COOK TIME: 15 minutes
SERVES 6
TEMPERATURE: 400°F

1 pound jumbo shrimp,
   peeled and deveined
2 medium zucchini, cut
   into ½-inch slices, then
   cut in half
2 bell peppers (red, yellow,
   or orange), cut into
   1-inch chunks
2 tablespoons Cajun
   seasoning
2 tablespoons extra-virgin
   olive oil, plus more for
   the basket
2 fully cooked smoked
   turkey sausages, cut into
   ½-inch slices

1. Preheat the air fryer to 400°F.

2. In a large bowl, toss the shrimp, zucchini, and bell peppers with the Cajun seasoning and olive oil. Stir in the smoked sausage slices.

3. Lightly spray the air fryer basket with oil. Place the seasoned shrimp, vegetables, and sausages in a single layer in the basket. (Air fry in batches, if necessary.)

4. Air fry for 15 minutes, shaking the basket every 5 minutes, until the vegetables are tender and seared and the sausage is crispy and lightly browned.

PER SERVING: Calories: 139; Total fat: 4g; Saturated fat: 1g; Cholesterol: 131mg; Sodium: 247mg; Carbohydrates: 4g; Fiber: 2g; Protein: 21g

Lobster Tails with Butter and Lemon

Lobster tails may sound difficult, but they are actually extremely easy to prepare. Cooking them in the air fryer is quick and lets you get a delicious, indulgent meal on the table in minutes.

GLUTEN-FREE, 30 MINUTES
OR LESS

PREP TIME: 10 minutes
COOK TIME: 10 minutes
SERVES 2
TEMPERATURE: 400°F

2 lobster tails
Extra-virgin olive oil, for greasing the basket
2 tablespoons butter, melted, plus more for serving (optional)
Salt
1 lemon, cut into wedges

1. Preheat the air fryer to 400°F.

2. Use kitchen scissors to cut the lobster tails from open end to the tail fins. Do not cut through the tail fins. Spread open the shell with your fingers and push the meat upward so it separates from the bottom shell. Be sure to leave the end attached at the tail fin. Hold the lobster meat up and push the shell together under the meat. Rest the meat on the top of the shell. This is a butterflied lobster tail.

3. Lightly spray the air fryer basket with oil. Place the lobster tails in a single layer in the basket. Pour the melted butter over the lobster meat and season with salt.

4. Air fry for 6 to 8 minutes, or until the shell is bright red, the lobster meat is white, and the internal temperature has reached 145°F.

5. Serve with lemon wedges and extra melted butter, if using.

PER SERVING: Calories: 192; Total fat: 13g; Saturated fat: 7g; Cholesterol: 176mg; Sodium: 311mg; Carbohydrates: 0g; Fiber: 0g; Protein: 19g

Crispy Fried Shrimp

You will be surprised how crispy these shrimp get with just a light spritz of extra-virgin olive oil. Fried shrimp pair nicely with Baby Potatoes (page 186), which you can also roast in the air fryer.

30 MINUTES OR LESS

PREP TIME: 15 minutes
COOK TIME: 15 minutes
SERVES 4
TEMPERATURE: 380°F

2 teaspoons Old Bay
   seasoning, divided
½ teaspoon garlic powder
½ teaspoon onion powder
½ teaspoon freshly ground
   black pepper
1 pound large shrimp,
   deveined, tails on
2 large eggs
1 teaspoon water
½ cup panko bread crumbs
Extra-virgin olive oil, for
   spraying

1. Preheat the air fryer to 380°F.

2. In a medium bowl, mix together 1 teaspoon Old Bay, the garlic powder, onion powder, and pepper. Add the shrimp and toss to lightly coat.

3. In a small bowl, whisk the eggs with the water.

4. In a second small shallow bowl, mix together the remaining 1 teaspoon Old Bay and the bread crumbs.

5. Coat each shrimp in the egg mixture, then the breading.

6. Lightly spray the air fryer basket with oil. Place the shrimp in a single layer in the basket. Do not overcrowd. (Air fry in batches, if necessary.) Lightly spray with oil.

7. Air fry for 10 to 15 minutes, shaking the basket every 5 minutes, until the shrimp are lightly browned and crispy.

Variation: You can use gluten-free panko bread crumbs to make this a gluten-free recipe.

PER SERVING: Calories: 197; Total fat: 5g; Saturated fat: 1g; Cholesterol: 248mg; Sodium: 538mg; Carbohydrates: 9g; Fiber: <1g; Protein: 27g

Fried Catfish

Air frying is a wonderful way to prepare this freshwater fish, and it's a much healthier option that the traditional method. The fish is first soaked in buttermilk to minimize any overly fishy flavors, then it's coated in cornmeal and Creole seasoning, both of which lend a wonderful texture and flavor.

GLUTEN-FREE

PREP TIME: 10 minutes, plus 1 hour to marinate

COOK TIME: 20 minutes

SERVES 4

TEMPERATURE: 400°F

1 cup buttermilk
4 catfish fillets
1 cup cornmeal
1 tablespoon Creole seasoning
Extra-virgin olive oil, for spraying

1. Pour the buttermilk into a shallow baking dish. Place the catfish in the dish, cover, and refrigerate for at least 1 hour.

2. Preheat the air fryer to 400°F.

3. In a small shallow bowl, combine the cornmeal and Creole seasoning.

4. Take the catfish out of the dish and shake off any excess buttermilk. Place each fillet in the cornmeal mixture. Press on the cornmeal to ensure it adheres.

5. Lightly spray the air fryer basket with oil. Place the coated catfish strips in a single layer in the basket. Lightly spray with oil.

6. Air fry for 7 to 10 minutes. Flip the catfish and lightly spray with oil. Air fry for an additional 8 to 10 minutes, or until golden brown and crispy.

Variation: If you do not have Creole seasoning on hand you can substitute Old Bay seasoning or Cajun seasoning.

PER SERVING: Calories: 288; Total fat: 11g; Saturated fat: 3g; Cholesterol: 67mg; Sodium: 210mg; Carbohydrates: 26g; Fiber: 2g; Protein: 21g

Chile-Lime Tilapia

I love that tilapia does not have a strong fishy flavor or odor. It is also inexpensive and easy to find. You can use fresh or frozen in this recipe. Air fried tilapia is tender and flaky, and the chile, cumin, and lime give this humble fish a whole new level of flavor.

DAIRY-FREE, GLUTEN-FREE, 30 MINUTES OR LESS

PREP TIME: 10 minutes
COOK TIME: 15 minutes
SERVES 4
TEMPERATURE: 380°F

4 teaspoons chili powder
2 teaspoons ground cumin
2 teaspoons garlic powder
1 teaspoon salt
½ teaspoon freshly ground black pepper
4 (5- to 6-ounce) tilapia fillets
Extra-virgin olive oil, for the parchment paper
2 limes, cut into wedges

1. Preheat the air fryer to 380°F.

2. In a small bowl, combine the chili powder, cumin, garlic powder, salt, and pepper.

3. Pat the tilapia fillets dry with a paper towel.

4. Press the spice mixture all over the fish.

5. Line the air fryer basket with a sheet of perforated parchment paper. Lightly spray the parchment with oil. Place the seasoned fillets in a single layer in the basket, leaving ½ inch of space between each to ensure even cooking. (Air fry in batches, if necessary.)

6. Air fry for 10 to 15 minutes, or until the fish is cooked through and flakes easily with a fork.

7. Drizzle lime juice over the top and serve.

Air Frying Tip: The cook time will depend on the thickness of the tilapia fillets. If you use a thicker fillet, you will need to add a few more minutes. Tilapia is very fragile, so avoid flipping it or the fish may break. The perforated parchment paper allows the fish to cook without being turned over.

PER SERVING: Calories: 131; Total fat: 3g; Saturated fat: 1g; Cholesterol: 57mg; Sodium: 1,086mg; Carbohydrates: 3g; Fiber: 2g; Protein: 26g

Bacon-Wrapped Scallops

Scallops wrapped in bacon are out-of-this-world delicious. With an air fryer you can make this delicacy in minutes. The bacon forms a ring that provides a crispy counterpoint to the tender, sweet, and buttery scallops. The bacon also contributes all the saltiness you need for this dish, so no extra is added.

DAIRY-FREE, GLUTEN-FREE,
30 MINUTES OR LESS

PREP TIME: 5 minutes
COOK TIME: 10 minutes
SERVES 4
TEMPERATURE: 400°F

1 pound jumbo sea scallops
1 pound sliced bacon
Extra-virgin olive oil, for
   the basket
Freshly ground black pepper

1. Preheat the air fryer to 400°F.

2. Pat the scallops dry with paper towels and remove any side muscles.

3. Cut the bacon slices in half so you have half a slice for each scallop.

4. Wrap each scallop in bacon and secure the bacon with a toothpick.

5. Lightly spray the air fryer basket with oil. Place the bacon-wrapped scallops in a single layer in the basket. (Air fry in batches, if necessary.)

6. Air fry for 8 minutes. Flip the scallops and season with pepper. Air fry for an additional 4 minutes, or until the bacon is cooked and crisped to your liking and the scallops are tender and opaque.

PER SERVING: Calories: 631; Total fat: 41g; Saturated fat: 14g; Cholesterol: 147mg; Sodium: 2,090mg; Carbohydrates: 5g; Fiber: 0g; Protein: 58g

Lemon-Garlic Jumbo Scallops

The flavors of garlic, lemon, and butter go perfectly with mild scallops, which cook quickly and wonderfully in the air fryer. Pair with steamed vegetables for a quick dinner, or they are perfect with a salad if you need a fast lunch.

GLUTEN-FREE, 30 MINUTES OR LESS

PREP TIME: 10 minutes
COOK TIME: 10 minutes
SERVES 4
TEMPERATURE: 400°F

4 tablespoons unsalted butter, melted
2 tablespoons freshly squeezed lemon juice
1 tablespoon minced garlic
½ teaspoon salt
⅛ teaspoon freshly ground black pepper
1 pound jumbo sea scallops
Extra-virgin olive oil, for the basket

1. Preheat the air fryer to 400°F.

2. In a medium bowl, combine the melted butter, lemon juice, garlic, salt, and pepper.

3. Add the sea scallops and toss to coat.

4. Lightly spray the air fryer basket with oil. Place the scallops in a single layer in the basket.

5. Air fry for 8 minutes, flipping after 4 minutes, until the scallops are opaque.

PER SERVING: Calories: 207; Total fat: 13g; Saturated fat: 7g; Cholesterol: 66mg; Sodium: 566mg; Carbohydrates: 4g; Fiber: 0g; Protein: 19g

Garlic-Ginger Salmon

Salmon is rich in omega-3 fatty acids, B vitamins, and potassium. It is a very versatile seafood, and pairs well with many different kinds of marinades. This simple garlic-ginger marinade infuses inviting aromas and delicious flavor. This salmon tastes great with sticky rice and freshly steamed vegetables.

DAIRY-FREE

PREP TIME: 10 minutes, plus up to 3 hours to marinate
COOK TIME: 10 minutes
SERVES 4
TEMPERATURE: 360°F

¼ cup soy sauce
2 tablespoons extra-virgin olive oil, plus more for the parchment paper
2 tablespoons grated fresh ginger
1 tablespoon minced garlic
1 tablespoon balsamic vinegar
4 (4-ounce) boneless, skinless salmon fillets

1. In a medium bowl, whisk together the soy sauce, olive oil, ginger, garlic, and balsamic vinegar.

2. Put the salmon in the marinade, cover, and refrigerate for at least 30 minutes but no longer than 3 hours.

3. Preheat the air fryer to 360°F.

4. Place a sheet of air fryer perforated parchment paper in the air fryer basket and lightly spray with oil. Place the marinated salmon fillets in a single layer in the basket.

5. Air fry for 6 minutes. Flip the fillets and air fry for an additional 4 to 6 minutes, or until the salmon is fully cooked and has reached an internal temperature of 145°F.

Air Frying Tip: The cook time will vary based on the size and thickness of the salmon fillet. If you want your salmon well-done, add a few more minutes.

PER SERVING: Calories: 214; Total fat: 11g; Saturated fat: 3g; Cholesterol: 55mg; Sodium: 1,048mg; Carbohydrates: 4g; Fiber: <1g; Protein: 24g

Fish and Chips

The best fish and chips I have ever eaten was in Gibraltar many years ago. It was delicious but loaded with fat and oil. Making this version of Fish and Chips in the air fryer is a much healthier option. Enjoy this recipe, which is inspired by the best version I've had to date.

DAIRY-FREE

PREP TIME: 25 minutes
COOK TIME: 35 minutes
SERVES 4
TEMPERATURE: 400°F

For the chips

2 large russet potatoes, scrubbed
1 tablespoon extra-virgin olive oil, plus more for greasing the basket
1 teaspoon seasoned salt
½ teaspoon freshly ground black pepper

INGREDIENTS CONTINUED ON PAGE 168

To make the chips

1. Preheat the air fryer to 400°F.

2. Cut the potatoes lengthwise into ½-inch-thick slices and then again into ½-inch-thick fries.

3. In a large bowl, mix the olive oil with the seasoned salt and pepper, then add the fries and toss to coat.

4. Lightly spray the air fryer basket with oil. Place the fries in a single layer in the basket. (Air fry in batches, if necessary.)

5. Air fry for 5 minutes. Shake the basket and air fry for an additional 5 to 10 minutes, or until lightly browned and crisp. Set aside and keep warm.

To make the fish

6. Season the fish fillets with salt and black pepper.

7. In a small shallow bowl, mix together the flour, ½ teaspoon salt, and ½ teaspoon black pepper.

8. In a second small shallow bowl, whisk together the eggs and a pinch each of salt and black pepper.

9. In a third small shallow bowl, combine the bread crumbs, cayenne pepper, remaining 1 teaspoon salt, and remaining 1 teaspoon black pepper.

CONTINUED

For the fish

4 (4-ounce) white fish fillets, such as pollock, cod, or haddock

1½ teaspoons salt, divided, plus more for seasoning

1½ teaspoons black pepper, divided, plus more for seasoning

½ cup all-purpose flour

2 large eggs

1 teaspoon water

1½ cups panko bread crumbs

¼ teaspoon cayenne pepper

Extra-virgin olive oil, for spraying

10. Preheat the air fryer to 400°F.

11. Coat each fillet in the seasoned flour, then in the egg, then in the breading.

12. Lightly spray the air fryer basket with oil. Place the coated fillets in a single layer in the basket. Lightly spray with oil.

13. Air fry for 8 to 10 minutes. Flip the fillets and lightly spray with oil. Air fry for an additional 5 to 10 minutes, or until golden brown and crispy.

Air Frying Tip: If you have trouble with your fish fillets sticking to the fryer basket, use air fryer-specific perforated parchment paper.

PER SERVING: Calories: 464; Total fat: 7g; Saturated fat: 2g; Cholesterol: 141mg; Sodium: 1,414mg; Carbohydrates: 69g; Fiber: 4g; Protein: 31g

Cod Nuggets

Eating these Cod Nuggets dipped in ketchup will make you feel like a kid again. Tartar sauce is another great option. If you do not have cod on hand, you can use any firm white fish for this classic recipe.

DAIRY-FREE, 30 MINUTES OR LESS

PREP TIME: 15 minutes
COOK TIME: 15 minutes
SERVES 4
TEMPERATURE: 400°F

4 (4-ounce) cod fillets
½ cup all-purpose flour
1 teaspoon seasoned salt
2 large eggs
1 teaspoon water
1½ cups panko bread crumbs
½ tablespoon dried parsley
1 teaspoon lemon-pepper seasoning
Extra-virgin olive oil, for spraying

1. Cut the cod fillets into 1-inch chunks.

2. In a small shallow bowl, mix together the flour and seasoned salt.

3. In a second small shallow bowl, whisk together the eggs and water.

4. In a third small shallow bowl, mix together the bread crumbs, parsley, and lemon-pepper seasoning.

5. Preheat the air fryer to 400°F.

6. Coat each cod chunk in the seasoned flour, then in the egg, then in the breading.

7. Lightly spray the air fryer basket with oil. Place the nuggets in a single layer in the basket. (Air fry in batches, if necessary.) Lightly spray with oil.

8. Air fry for 7 minutes. Flip the nuggets and lightly spray with oil. Air fry for an additional 6 to 8 minutes, or until fully cooked, golden brown, and crispy.

Variation: If you prefer fish sticks instead of fish nuggets, cut the cod fillets lengthwise into strips instead of chunks. The cook time will remain the same.

PER SERVING: Calories: 263; Total fat: 1g; Saturated fat: <1g; Cholesterol: 96mg; Sodium: 615mg; Carbohydrates: 35g; Fiber: 1g; Protein: 23g

Breaded Calamari

I still remember when my dad took me out for a nice seafood dinner for my 16th birthday. It was my first time trying breaded calamari, and I was hooked. It's still one of my favorite appetizers to order at restaurants, but I really love being able to make this dish at home, knowing it is not loaded with oil and grease. Breaded Calamari are great dipped in ranch dressing or marinara sauce.

DAIRY-FREE, 30 MINUTES OR LESS

PREP TIME: 15 minutes
COOK TIME: 15 minutes
SERVES 4
TEMPERATURE: 380°F

1 pound fresh calamari tubes, rinsed and patted dry
½ teaspoon salt, plus more for seasoning
½ teaspoon freshly ground black pepper, plus more for seasoning
1 cup all-purpose flour
3 large eggs
1 teaspoon water
1 cup panko bread crumbs
2 teaspoons dried parsley
Extra-virgin olive oil, for spraying

1. Cut the calamari into ¼-inch rings. Season with salt and pepper.

2. In a small shallow bowl, combine the flour, salt, and pepper.

3. In a second small shallow bowl, whisk together the eggs and water.

4. In a third small shallow bowl, combine the bread crumbs and parsley.

5. Preheat the air fryer to 380°F.

6. Coat the calamari rings in the seasoned flour, then in the egg, then in the breading.

7. Lightly spray the air fryer basket with oil. Place the breaded calamari in a single layer in the basket. (Air fry in batches, if necessary.) Lightly spray with oil.

8. Air fry for 10 to 15 minutes, shaking the basket a few times, until lightly browned and crispy.

Air Frying Tip: You can use frozen calamari, but be sure to thaw and pat dry prior to using.

PER SERVING: Calories: 287; Total fat: 4g; Saturated fat: 1g; Cholesterol: 239mg; Sodium: 831mg; Carbohydrates: 40g; Fiber: 2g; Protein: 22g

Coconut Shrimp

Coconut Shrimp are the perfect blend of sweet and savory and make a delicious appetizer or main dish. They taste amazing dipped in sweet chili sauce and are great with steamed or air fried vegetables on the side.

DAIRY-FREE, 30 MINUTES OR LESS

PREP TIME: 20 minutes
COOK TIME: 10 minutes
SERVES 4
TEMPERATURE: 370°F

½ cup all-purpose flour
½ teaspoon salt
¼ teaspoon freshly ground black pepper
2 large eggs
Dash hot sauce
1 cup sweetened shredded coconut
½ cup panko bread crumbs
1 pound large uncooked shrimp, peeled and deveined
Extra-virgin olive oil, for spraying

1. In a small shallow bowl, combine the flour, salt, and pepper.

2. In a second small shallow bowl, whisk together the eggs and hot sauce.

3. In a third small shallow bowl, combine the coconut and bread crumbs.

4. Preheat the air fryer to 370°F.

5. Lightly coat the shrimp in the flour mixture, then in the egg mixture, allowing the excess to drip off. Coat the shrimp in the coconut breading. Press on the breading to ensure it adheres.

6. Lightly spray the air fryer basket with oil. Place the coated shrimp in a single layer in the basket. (Air fry in batches, if necessary.) Lightly spray with oil.

7. Air fry for 5 minutes. Gently flip the shrimp and lightly spray with oil. Air fry for an additional 4 to 5 minutes, or until lightly browned and crispy.

PER SERVING: Calories: 384; Total fat: 18g; Saturated fat: 12g; Cholesterol: 248mg; Sodium: 520mg; Carbohydrates: 26g; Fiber: 4g; Protein: 30g

Crispy Ranch Haddock Fillets

Haddock is a saltwater fish in the cod family. This mild, slightly sweet fish is simple to bread and air fry. Dry ranch dressing mix brings a bright and savory flavor to the crispy breading. Serve with Onion Rings (page 79) for a fast lunch or dinner.

30 MINUTES OR LESS

PREP TIME: 10 minutes

COOK TIME: 10 minutes

SERVES 4

TEMPERATURE: 350°F

½ cup all-purpose flour
½ teaspoon salt
½ teaspoon freshly ground black pepper
2 large eggs
1½ cups panko bread crumbs
2 tablespoons dry ranch dressing mix
4 (4-ounce) haddock fillets
Extra-virgin olive oil, for spraying

1. In a small shallow bowl, combine the flour, salt, and pepper.

2. In a second small shallow bowl, whisk the eggs.

3. In a third small shallow bowl, combine the bread crumbs and ranch dressing mix.

4. Preheat the air fryer to 350°F.

5. Lightly coat the haddock fillets in the flour mixture, then in the egg, allowing the excess to drip off. Coat the haddock pieces in the breading. Press on the breading to ensure it adheres.

6. Lightly spray the air fryer basket with oil. Place the coated fillets in a single layer in the basket. (Air fry in batches, if necessary.) Lightly spray with oil.

7. Air-fry for 8 minutes. Gently flip the haddock fillets and lightly spray with oil. Air fry for an additional 4 minutes, or until lightly browned and crispy.

Air Frying Tip: If the fish fillets stick to the basket, put down a sheet of air fryer-specific perforated parchment paper.

....

PER SERVING: Calories: 301; Total fat: 3g; Saturated fat: 1g; Cholesterol: 154mg; Sodium: 630mg; Carbohydrates: 38g; Fiber: 1g; Protein: 26g

Zesty Fish Cakes

Forget standard fish cakes; you'll love this more flavorful version. Even though this is already a quick meal, you can save more time by making the patties ahead and refrigerating them until you are ready to air fry. Serve with a big garden salad for a light and healthy meal.

30 MINUTES OR LESS

PREP TIME: 10 minutes
COOK TIME: 10 minutes
SERVES 4
TEMPERATURE: 380°F

2 (5-ounce) cans solid white albacore tuna in water, drained

1 large egg, beaten

1½ cups panko bread crumbs, divided

3 tablespoons finely chopped cilantro

2 tablespoons sweet chili sauce

2 tablespoons oyster sauce

2 teaspoons minced garlic

¼ teaspoon cayenne pepper

½ teaspoon salt

½ teaspoon freshly ground black pepper

Extra-virgin olive oil, for spraying

1. In a medium bowl, combine the tuna, egg, ¾ cup bread crumbs, cilantro, chili sauce, oyster sauce, garlic, and cayenne pepper. Stir the ingredients lightly with a fork until well mixed, but with some intact tuna chunks for texture.

2. In a small shallow bowl, combine the remaining ¾ cup bread crumbs, the salt, and black pepper.

3. Preheat the air fryer to 380°F.

4. Use a 2- to 3-ounce ice cream scoop to form the tuna mixture into equal-size patties. Coat each patty with the breading.

5. Lightly spray the air fryer basket with oil. Place the fish cakes in a single layer in the basket. (Air fry in batches, if necessary.) Lightly spray with oil.

6. Air fry for 4 minutes. Gently flip the fish cakes and lightly spray with oil. Air fry for an additional 4 minutes, or until golden brown and crispy.

PER SERVING: Calories: 236; Total fat: 3g; Saturated fat: 1g; Cholesterol: 74mg; Sodium: 923mg; Carbohydrates: 27g; Fiber: 1g; Protein: 20g

CHAPTER 8

Vegetable Sides and Mains

Creole Carrot Fries

Carrot fries are addictive. You get a slight sweetness in each bite combined with the heat from the Creole seasoning that keeps you coming back for more. I recommend making some spicy ketchup for dipping by adding a squirt of sriracha to your regular ketchup.

GLUTEN-FREE, VEGAN, 30 MINUTES OR LESS

PREP TIME: 10 minutes
COOK TIME: 20 minutes
SERVES 4
TEMPERATURE: 350°F

1 pound carrots, peeled and cut into ¼-inch matchsticks
2 tablespoons cornstarch
2 tablespoons extra-virgin olive oil, plus more for the parchment paper
2 teaspoons sugar
1 teaspoon Creole seasoning

1. Preheat the air fryer to 350°F.

2. In a large bowl, toss the carrots with the cornstarch until well coated.

3. Add the olive oil and toss to coat.

4. Sprinkle the sugar and Creole seasoning over the carrots and toss to coat.

5. Place a sheet of air fryer parchment paper in the air fryer basket and lightly spray with oil. Place the carrots in a single layer in the basket on the parchment paper. (Air fry in batches, if necessary.)

6. Air fry for 15 to 20 minutes, shaking the basket every 5 minutes, until the carrots start to get brown and crispy.

Air Frying Tip: Air fried carrots should be eaten while hot. They may get soft if left to cool for too long.

Variation: If you do not have Creole seasoning on hand, you can use Cajun seasoning instead.

PER SERVING: Calories: 130; Total fat: 7g; Saturated fat: 1g; Cholesterol: 0mg; Sodium: 79mg; Carbohydrates: 17g; Fiber: 3g; Protein: 1g

Prosciutto-Wrapped Asparagus

This elegant side dish is a classic Italian pairing, perfect for holiday meals or entertaining. There is no need to add extra salt or seasonings to the spears because the prosciutto is bursting with flavor.

DAIRY-FREE, GLUTEN-FREE, 30 MINUTES OR LESS

PREP TIME: 10 minutes
COOK TIME: 10 minutes
SERVES 4
TEMPERATURE: 350°F

12 asparagus spears, ends trimmed

6 slices prosciutto, cut in half

1 teaspoon extra-virgin olive oil, divided, plus more for the basket

1. Preheat the air fryer to 350°F.

2. Wrap each asparagus spear with a piece of prosciutto. Brush the ends of each spear with olive oil.

3. Lightly spray the air fryer basket with oil. Place the wrapped asparagus spears in a single layer in the basket.

4. Air fry for 5 to 8 minutes, or until the prosciutto is cooked and lightly browned and the spears are tender.

Air Frying Tip: Brushing the ends of the asparagus with olive oil will help prevent the ends from burning and drying out during cooking.

PER SERVING: Calories: 72; Total fat: 5g; Saturated fat: 2g; Cholesterol: 23mg; Sodium: 519mg; Carbohydrates: 3g; Fiber: 1g; Protein: 7g

Lemon-Garlic Green Beans and Mushrooms

Fresh green beans are delicious in the air fryer as well as exceedingly healthy. This versatile vegetable cooks quickly, brings color to the plate, and pairs perfectly with mushrooms. This is a great side for Boneless Pork Chops (page 128).

DAIRY-FREE, GLUTEN-FREE, VEGAN, 30 MINUTES OR LESS

PREP TIME: 5 minutes
COOK TIME: 10 minutes
SERVES 4
TEMPERATURE: 390°F

1 pound green
   beans, trimmed
8 ounces button
   mushrooms, cut
   into thirds
¼ cup extra-virgin olive oil,
   plus more for the basket
2 tablespoons freshly
   squeezed lemon juice
1 tablespoon minced garlic
Salt
Freshly ground black pepper

1. Preheat the air fryer to 390°F.

2. In a large bowl, toss the green beans, mushrooms, olive oil, lemon juice, garlic, salt, and pepper.

3. Lightly spray the air fryer basket with oil. Place the green beans and mushrooms in the basket.

4. Air fry for 10 minutes, shaking the basket after 5 minutes, until the green beans begin to look light brown on the ends and are tender-crisp.

Variation: You can add a ½ teaspoon of red pepper flakes in step 2 to increase the heat in this recipe.

PER SERVING: Calories: 172; Total fat: 14g; Saturated fat: 2g; Cholesterol: 0mg; Sodium: 10mg; Carbohydrates: 11g; Fiber: 4g; Protein: 4g

Loaded Corn Fritters

Corn fritters are a favorite of mine from childhood. This version adds a bit of spice from the pepper Jack cheese and reduces the oil needed to get a crispy fritter. They are wonderful on their own, dipped in sour cream, or with your choice of dressing.

PREP TIME: 10 minutes, plus 30 minutes to chill
COOK TIME: 15 minutes
SERVES 5
TEMPERATURE: 400°F

2 large eggs
1 teaspoon salt
1 teaspoon baking powder
½ teaspoon freshly ground black pepper
½ cup all-purpose flour
1 (15-ounce) can corn, drained
¾ cup shredded pepper Jack cheese
¼ cup crumbled cooked bacon
½ teaspoon dry parsley
Extra-virgin olive oil, for the basket

1. Line a baking sheet with parchment paper.

2. In a large bowl, combine the eggs, salt, baking powder, and pepper. Add the flour and whisk until a thick batter forms.

3. Stir in the corn, cheese, bacon, and parsley.

4. Scoop ¼ cup of the batter and form it into a patty. Place the patty on the prepared baking sheet. Repeat with the remaining batter.

5. Place the baking sheet in the freezer for 30 minutes so the fritters will hold their shape during cooking.

6. Preheat the air fryer to 400°F.

7. Lightly spray the air fryer basket with oil. Place the corn fritters in a single layer in the basket, leaving about ½ inch of space between each to ensure even cooking.

8. Air fry for 8 minutes. Gently flip the fritters and air fry for 5 to 7 additional minutes, or until golden brown and cooked through.

PER SERVING: Calories: 195; Total fat: 10g; Saturated fat: 5g; Cholesterol: 86mg; Sodium: 878mg; Carbohydrates: 19g; Fiber: 2g; Protein: 10g

Crispy Brussels Sprouts with Almonds

Brussels sprouts are a healthy vegetable that always turns out perfect when air fried. The almonds add a nice crunch to this side dish that pairs well with turkey, chicken, pork, or beef. It's also wonderful on top of a salad.

DAIRY-FREE, GLUTEN-FREE, VEGAN, 30 MINUTES OR LESS

PREP TIME: 10 minutes
COOK TIME: 10 minutes
SERVES 4
TEMPERATURE: 350°F

2 tablespoons extra-virgin olive oil, plus more for the basket

2 tablespoons red wine vinegar

2 teaspoons dried parsley

⅛ teaspoon salt

⅛ teaspoon freshly ground black pepper

⅛ teaspoon red pepper flakes

1 pound Brussels sprouts, trimmed with outer leaves removed and cut in half

3 tablespoons roasted sliced almonds

1. Preheat the air fryer to 350°F.

2. In a medium bowl, whisk together the olive oil, red wine vinegar, parsley, salt, black pepper, and red pepper flakes.

3. Add the Brussels sprouts and almonds and toss to coat.

4. Lightly spray the air fryer basket with oil. Place the coated sprouts and almonds in the basket.

5. Air fry for 8 to 10 minutes, shaking the basket halfway through, until tender and lightly browned along the edges.

PER SERVING: Calories: 144; Total fat: 10g; Saturated fat: 1g; Cholesterol: 0mg; Sodium: 69mg; Carbohydrates: 11g; Fiber: 5g; Protein: 5g

Balsamic-Soy Roasted Mushrooms

This dish is heavenly for mushroom lovers because the marinade enhances the mushrooms' natural taste and highlights all their rich, earthy flavors. Serve with steak for an unbeatable pairing.

DAIRY-FREE, GLUTEN-FREE, VEGAN, 30 MINUTES OR LESS

PREP TIME: 5 minutes
COOK TIME: 10 minutes
SERVES 4
TEMPERATURE: 390°F

3 tablespoons balsamic vinegar

1½ tablespoons soy sauce

1 tablespoon extra-virgin olive oil, plus more for spraying

½ tablespoon brown sugar

1 tablespoon minced garlic

½ teaspoon dried thyme

½ teaspoon freshly ground black pepper

2 pounds whole button mushrooms

1. Preheat the air fryer to 390°F.

2. In a large bowl, combine the balsamic vinegar, soy sauce, olive oil, brown sugar, garlic, thyme, and pepper.

3. Add the mushrooms and toss to combine.

4. Lightly spray the air fryer basket with oil. Place the mushrooms in a single layer in the basket. Lightly spray with oil.

5. Air fry for 10 minutes, shaking the basket and lightly spraying with oil halfway through, until tender.

Air Frying Tip: Mushrooms will not get crisp in the air fryer. They end up tender with an amazing roasted texture.

PER SERVING: Calories: 102; Total fat: 4g; Saturated fat: 1g; Cholesterol: 0mg; Sodium: 343mg; Carbohydrates: 11g; Fiber: 2g; Protein: 8g

Artichoke Hearts

Change up your vegetable side dish with some tender and flavorful artichoke hearts. The clean, earthy taste of Artichoke Hearts will please your taste buds. Using canned artichokes will save you a lot of time. Serve with steak, chicken, or a salad.

GLUTEN-FREE, 30 MINUTES OR LESS

PREP TIME: 10 minutes
COOK TIME: 10 minutes
SERVES 4
TEMPERATURE: 390°F

2 (14-ounce) cans quartered artichoke hearts in water, drained
1½ tablespoons grated Parmesan cheese
¾ teaspoon Italian seasoning
½ teaspoon salt
½ teaspoon freshly ground black pepper
¼ teaspoon garlic powder
Extra-virgin olive oil, for spraying

1. Preheat the air fryer to 390°F.

2. Gently pat dry the artichoke hearts with a paper towel.

3. In a medium bowl, combine the Parmesan cheese, Italian seasoning, salt, pepper, and garlic powder.

4. Add the artichokes to the bowl and stir gently to coat.

5. Lightly spray the air fryer basket with oil. Place the artichokes in a single layer in the basket. Lightly spray with oil.

6. Air fry for 8 minutes, shaking the basket a few times to redistribute, until the artichokes start to brown and are tender with crispy edges.

PER SERVING: Calories: 73; Total fat: 1g; Saturated fat: <1g; Cholesterol: 2mg; Sodium: 845mg; Carbohydrates: 18g; Fiber: 14g; Protein: 6g

Roasted Beet Chips

The sweet yet savory flavors of roasted beet chips may surprise you. Air frying the beets at a lower temperature allows them to crisp up without burning the edges. It's a delicious and healthy snack or side dish you'll keep coming back to.

DAIRY-FREE, GLUTEN-FREE, VEGAN, 30 MINUTES OR LESS

PREP TIME: 10 minutes
COOK TIME: 20 minutes
SERVES 4
TEMPERATURE: 330°F

3 beet roots, peeled
1 tablespoon extra-virgin olive oil, plus more for greasing the basket
1 teaspoon seasoned salt
½ teaspoon freshly ground black pepper

1. Preheat the air fryer to 330°F.

2. Using a mandoline, cut the beets into $1/16$-inch slices.

3. In a large bowl, toss the beet slices with the olive oil, seasoned salt, and pepper.

4. Lightly spray the air fryer basket with oil. Place the beet slices in a single layer in the basket. It's okay if they overlap a little.

5. Air fry for 15 to 20 minutes, stirring and separating the slices every 5 minutes, until slightly crispy.

6. Let the beet chips rest for a few minutes. They will crisp up more during this time.

Air Frying Tip: It may be tempting to continue cooking the beets until they appear very crispy, but doing so will result in a burnt flavor. Stop cooking when they are only slightly crispy.

PER SERVING: Calories: 58; Total fat: 4g; Saturated fat: 1g; Cholesterol: 0mg; Sodium: 390mg; Carbohydrates: 6g; Fiber: 2g; Protein: 1g

Baby Potatoes

This go-to side dish is tasty and a nice complement to a variety of dishes. The bold flavors of chili powder and paprika turn plain potatoes into a flavorful side that goes great with practically any main dish. Try them with Garlic Turkey Burgers (page 99) or Breaded Calamari (page 170) for a filling dinner.

DAIRY-FREE, GLUTEN-FREE, VEGAN, 30 MINUTES OR LESS

PREP TIME: 5 minutes
COOK TIME: 15 minutes
SERVES 4
TEMPERATURE: 400°F

1 tablespoon minced garlic
2 teaspoons chili powder
1 teaspoon salt
½ teaspoon smoked paprika
¼ teaspoon cayenne pepper
1 pound baby potatoes, scrubbed
1 tablespoon extra-virgin olive oil, plus more for the basket

1. Preheat the air fryer to 400°F.

2. In a medium bowl, combine the garlic, chili powder, salt, paprika, and cayenne pepper. Add the potatoes and olive oil and toss.

3. Lightly spray the air fryer basket with oil. Place the coated potatoes in a single layer in the basket.

4. Air fry for 15 minutes, shaking the basket every 5 minutes to redistribute, until the potatoes are tender with a crispy peel.

Air Frying Tip: For extra crispy potatoes, spray more olive oil on the potatoes when you shake the basket.

PER SERVING: Calories: 125; Total fat: 4g; Saturated fat: 1g; Cholesterol: 0mg; Sodium: 642mg; Carbohydrates: 21g; Fiber: 2g; Protein: 2g

Mashed Potato Pancakes

Do not throw out your leftover mashed potatoes—you can turn them into crispy potato pancakes in the air fryer. They are excellent served with any meal or even as a midday snack. Try them with an aioli dipping sauce or sour cream on the side.

30 MINUTES OR LESS

PREP TIME: 10 minutes, plus 15 minutes to chill
COOK TIME: 10 minutes
SERVES 5
TEMPERATURE: 390°F

2 cups mashed potatoes
1 cup shredded Colby-Jack cheese
¼ cup crumbled cooked bacon
1 large egg
2 cups panko bread crumbs, divided
½ teaspoon Cajun seasoning
½ teaspoon salt
¼ teaspoon freshly ground black pepper
Extra-virgin olive oil, for the basket

1. Line a baking sheet with parchment paper.

2. In a large bowl, combine the mashed potatoes, cheese, bacon, egg, 1 cup bread crumbs, and Cajun seasoning.

3. Scoop ½ cup of the batter and form it into a patty. Repeat with the remaining batter. You should have about 5 patties.

4. In a small shallow bowl, combine the remaining 1 cup bread crumbs, salt, and pepper.

5. Coat each patty in the bread crumb mixture, then place it on the prepared baking sheet. Put the baking sheet in the freezer for 15 minutes so the patties will hold their shape during cooking.

6. Preheat the air fryer to 390°F.

7. Lightly spray the air fryer basket with oil. Place the coated potato pancakes in a single layer in the basket. Lightly spray with oil.

8. Air fry for 6 minutes. Flip the pancakes and lightly spray with oil. Air fry for an additional 4 to 6 minutes, or until golden brown and crispy.

Air Frying Tip: Use a spatula made of silicone, wood, or nylon so it doesn't scratch the basket's nonstick coating.

PER SERVING: Calories: 340; Total fat: 13g; Saturated fat: 6g; Cholesterol: 58mg; Sodium: 645mg; Carbohydrates: 42g; Fiber: 3g; Protein: 13g

Spicy Italian Zucchini Boats

Classic Italian flavors plus a hint of spice from the red pepper flakes are balanced with plenty of beautiful melted cheese on top. It's a healthy and fun way to use up fresh zucchini from the garden. Meatless Mondays have never tasted so good.

GLUTEN-FREE, 30 MINUTES OR LESS

PREP TIME: 15 minutes
COOK TIME: 15 minutes
SERVES 4
TEMPERATURE: 370°F

2 medium zucchini
¾ cup marinara sauce
½ cup chopped mushrooms
½ cup shredded
  Parmesan cheese
¼ cup finely chopped red
  bell pepper
1 teaspoon minced garlic
¾ teaspoon Italian
  seasoning
¼ teaspoon red
  pepper flakes
Extra-virgin olive oil, for
  spraying
Salt
Freshly ground black pepper
1 cup shredded
  mozzarella cheese

1. Cut the zucchini in half lengthwise and scoop out the middle of each half to create a boat. Reserve the zucchini pulp and chop it finely.

2. In a large bowl, combine the zucchini pulp, marinara sauce, mushrooms, Parmesan cheese, bell pepper, garlic, Italian seasoning, and red pepper flakes.

3. Preheat the air fryer to 370°F.

4. Lightly spray the zucchini halves with oil. Season with salt and black pepper. Divide the filling evenly among the four boats.

5. Lightly spray the air fryer basket with oil. Place the zucchini boats in a single layer in the basket.

6. Air fry for 10 minutes. Open the air fryer and sprinkle ¼ cup of mozzarella cheese on top of each zucchini boat. Air fry for an additional 2 to 3 minutes, or until the cheese has melted and is starting to crisp.

Air Frying Tip: If you have a smaller air fryer, try using a rack so you can cook more stuffed zucchini at the same time.

PER SERVING: Calories: 163; Total fat: 9g; Saturated fat: 5g; Cholesterol: 24mg; Sodium: 393mg; Carbohydrates: 11g; Fiber: 2g; Protein: 12g

Breaded Eggplant Slices

Adding breading to eggplant slices is a great way to get some crunch and additional flavor. The skin of the eggplant is totally edible, and leaving it on saves time and retains healthy nutrients and antioxidants. If you wish, serve with marinara and grated Parmesan for an easy take on eggplant parmigiana.

30 MINUTES OR LESS

PREP TIME: 15 minutes
COOK TIME: 10 minutes
SERVES 4
TEMPERATURE: 360°F

1 large eggplant
½ cup all-purpose flour
½ teaspoon salt
½ teaspoon freshly ground
   black pepper
2 large eggs
½ cup panko bread crumbs
¼ cup grated
   Parmesan cheese
½ teaspoon Cajun
   seasoning
Extra-virgin olive oil, for
   the basket
Marinara sauce, for serving
   (optional)

1. Cut the eggplant into ¼-inch-thick round slices.

2. In a small shallow bowl, combine the flour, salt, and pepper.

3. In a second small shallow bowl, whisk the eggs.

4. In a third small shallow bowl, combine the bread crumbs, Parmesan cheese, and Cajun seasoning.

5. Preheat the air fryer to 360°F.

6. Coat the eggplant slices in the flour mixture, then in the eggs, allowing any excess egg to drip off. Coat the slices in the breading.

7. Lightly spray the air fryer basket with oil. Place the coated eggplant slices in a single layer in the basket. (Air fry in batches, if necessary.) Lightly spray with oil.

8. Air fry for 6 minutes. Flip the slices and lightly spray with oil. Air fry for an additional 4 minutes, or until lightly browned and crispy.

9. Serve with marinara sauce for dipping, if desired.

Variation: If you do not care for the spice in Cajun seasoning, replace it with seasoned salt.

PER SERVING: Calories: 197; Total fat: 5g; Saturated fat: 2g; Cholesterol: 87mg; Sodium: 455mg; Carbohydrates: 31g; Fiber: 6g; Protein: 9g

Classic French Fries

French fries may have originated in Europe, but they have been completely embraced in America. The air fryer allows us to enjoy this guilty pleasure without nearly as much guilt! Even though this version uses much less oil, the fries still turn out nice and crispy.

DAIRY-FREE, GLUTEN-FREE, VEGAN, 30 MINUTES OR LESS

PREP TIME: 15 minutes
COOK TIME: 15 minutes
SERVES 4
TEMPERATURE: 400°F

4 large russet potatoes, scrubbed
1½ tablespoons extra-virgin olive oil, plus more for greasing the basket
2 teaspoons seasoned salt
1 teaspoon freshly ground black pepper

1. Preheat the air fryer to 400°F.

2. Cut the potatoes lengthwise into ½-inch-thick slices and then into ½-inch-thick fries.

3. In a large bowl, toss the potatoes with oil, seasoned salt, and pepper.

4. Lightly spray the air fryer basket with oil. Place the fries in a single layer in the basket. (Air fry in batches, if necessary.)

5. Air fry for 5 minutes. Shake the basket and air fry for an additional 5 to 10 minutes, or until lightly browned and crispy.

Air Frying Tip: Cook time will vary based on the thickness of the potato slices. If you like thick fries, add a few more minutes of cook time. If you prefer thin fries, reduce the cook time by a few minutes.

PER SERVING: Calories: 340; Total fat: 5g; Saturated fat: 1g; Cholesterol: 0mg; Sodium: 702mg; Carbohydrates: 67g; Fiber: 5g; Protein: 8g

Twice-Baked Potatoes

Twice-Baked Potatoes are a beloved side dish that is so filling it could almost be a meal on its own. Feel free to add some cooked and crumbled bacon to the mix if you want some additional protein and flavor.

GLUTEN-FREE, VEGETARIAN

PREP TIME: 15 minutes, plus 5 minutes to cool

COOK TIME: 40 minutes

SERVES 4

TEMPERATURE: 380°F and 400°F

4 large russet potatoes, scrubbed clean

Extra-virgin olive oil, for the basket

½ teaspoon salt, plus more for seasoning

½ teaspoon freshly ground black pepper, plus more for seasoning

1 cup sour cream

4 tablespoons unsalted butter, at room temperature

½ cup milk

2 scallions, thinly sliced

1½ cups shredded cheddar cheese, divided

1. Preheat the air fryer to 380°F.

2. Lightly spray the potatoes with oil and season with salt and pepper. Pierce the potatoes a few times with a fork.

3. Lightly spray the air fryer basket with oil. Place the potatoes in the basket.

4. Air fry for 30 minutes, or until fork-tender.

5. Let the potatoes cool enough to handle, about 5 minutes.

6. Cut the potatoes in half lengthwise. Use a spoon to scoop out the potato flesh, leaving ½ inch of flesh lining the inside of each potato half.

7. In a medium bowl, combine the scooped-out potato, sour cream, butter, milk, scallions, 1 cup cheese, the salt, and pepper.

8. Fill each potato half with ½ cup of the potato mixture.

9. Preheat the air fryer to 400°F.

10. Lightly spray the air fryer basket with oil. Place the potatoes in a single layer in the basket.

11. Air fry for 6 minutes. Sprinkle the remaining ½ cup cheese on top of the potato halves and air fry for an additional 2 to 3 minutes, or until the cheese has melted.

Air Frying Tip: There is no need to clean the fryer basket after cooking the baked potatoes.

PER SERVING: Calories: 700; Total fat: 38g; Saturated fat: 22g; Cholesterol: 109mg; Sodium: 713mg; Carbohydrates: 73g; Fiber: 5g; Protein: 20g

Buffalo Cauliflower Bites

If you love spicy buffalo sauce (or want a healthier alternative to buffalo chicken wings), you will love this recipe, which turns a healthy vegetable into an addictive side dish. These little Buffalo Cauliflower Bites taste amazing dipped in ranch or blue cheese dressing. Be warned: They don't last long at parties.

DAIRY-FREE, GLUTEN-FREE, VEGAN, 30 MINUTES OR LESS

PREP TIME: 10 minutes
COOK TIME: 15 minutes
SERVES 4
TEMPERATURE: 360°F

1 cup buffalo sauce
2 tablespoons extra-virgin olive oil, plus more for spraying
1 teaspoon honey
¾ teaspoon garlic powder
½ teaspoon salt
½ teaspoon freshly ground black pepper
1 head cauliflower, cut into bite-size florets
Ranch dressing, for serving (optional)

1. Preheat the air fryer to 360°F.

2. In a large bowl, combine the buffalo sauce, olive oil, honey, garlic powder, salt, and pepper.

3. Toss the cauliflower florets in the sauce to coat.

4. Lightly spray the air fryer basket with oil. Place the coated cauliflower bites in a single layer in the basket. (Air fry in batches, if necessary.)

5. Air fry for 15 minutes, shaking the basket halfway through and lightly spraying the florets with oil, until fork-tender and lightly browned.

6. Serve with ranch dressing for dipping, if desired.

Air Frying Tip: My experience with cauliflower in the air fryer is that it does not ever get truly crispy. Instead, it is more of a roasted, slightly crisp texture that is absolutely delicious!

PER SERVING: Calories: 177; Total fat: 14g; Saturated fat: 3g; Cholesterol: 0mg; Sodium: 1,119mg; Carbohydrates: 12g; Fiber: 4g; Protein: 3g

Fried Green Tomatoes

The tang of green tomatoes combined with crispy breading is a favorite for many, and a cornerstone of Southern cooking. It is possible to get a crispy, crunchy fried green tomato in the air fryer and save all the oil normally required for skillet frying.

VEGETARIAN, 30 MINUTES OR LESS

PREP TIME: 10 minutes
COOK TIME: 20 minutes
SERVES 4
TEMPERATURE: 360°F

2 large green tomatoes
½ cup all-purpose flour
½ teaspoon salt
½ teaspoon freshly ground black pepper
2 large eggs
2 tablespoons water
¾ cup cornmeal
¼ cup panko bread crumbs
½ teaspoon red pepper flakes
½ teaspoon garlic powder
Extra-virgin olive oil, for spraying
Ketchup or ranch dressing, for serving (optional)

1. Cut the tomatoes into ¼-inch-thick round slices.

2. In a small shallow bowl, combine the flour, salt, and black pepper.

3. In a second small shallow bowl, whisk together the eggs and water.

4. In a third small shallow bowl, combine the cornmeal, bread crumbs, red pepper flakes, and garlic powder.

5. Preheat the air fryer to 360°F.

6. Coat the tomato slices in the flour mixture, then in the eggs, allowing any excess egg to drip off. Coat the slices in the cornmeal breading.

7. Lightly spray the air fryer basket with oil. Place the coated tomato slices in a single layer in the basket. (Air fry in batches, if necessary.) Lightly spray with oil.

8. Air fry for 10 minutes. Flip the tomato slices and lightly spray with oil. Air fry for an additional 8 minutes, or until golden brown and crispy.

9. Serve with ketchup or ranch dressing for dipping, if desired.

PER SERVING: Calories: 215; Total fat: 4g; Saturated fat: 1g; Cholesterol: 82mg; Sodium: 350mg; Carbohydrates: 39g; Fiber: 3g; Protein: 8g

Parmesan Roasted Zucchini

This simple yet delicious side dish goes with almost any main course and is on the table in minutes. Pair with Bacon-Wrapped Scallops (page 162), Chicken Florentine Meatballs (page 101), or Spice-Rubbed T-Bone Steak (page 145).

GLUTEN-FREE, 30 MINUTES OR LESS

PREP TIME: 5 minutes
COOK TIME: 10 minutes
SERVES 4
TEMPERATURE: 400°F

3 medium zucchini
3 tablespoons extra-virgin olive oil, plus more for spraying
¼ cup grated Parmesan cheese
1 heaped teaspoon Italian seasoning
½ teaspoon salt
½ teaspoon freshly ground black pepper

1. Preheat the air fryer to 400°F.

2. Cut the zucchini in half lengthwise, then cut each half into ½-inch-thick slices (half moons).

3. In a large bowl, toss the zucchini with the olive oil, Parmesan cheese, Italian seasoning, salt, and pepper.

4. Lightly spray the air fryer basket with oil. Place the zucchini in a single layer in the basket. Lightly spray with oil. (Air fry in batches, if necessary.)

5. Air fry for 8 minutes, shaking the basket every 2 to 3 minutes and lightly spraying the zucchini with oil, until the zucchini is tender and begins to brown.

PER SERVING: Calories: 142; Total fat: 12g; Saturated fat: 3g; Cholesterol: 5mg; Sodium: 420mg; Carbohydrates: 6g; Fiber: 2g; Protein: 4g

Smoky Fried Cabbage

Traditional fried cabbage is fried in bacon grease or butter and is exceedingly high in fat. Try making it in the air fryer for a healthier version that tastes amazing. You'll love the smokiness this dish gets from the addition of smoked paprika.

DAIRY-FREE, GLUTEN-FREE, VEGAN, 30 MINUTES OR LESS

PREP TIME: 5 minutes
COOK TIME: 15 minutes
SERVES 4
TEMPERATURE: 400°F

1 head green cabbage
2 tablespoons extra-virgin olive oil, plus more for spraying
2 tablespoons apple cider vinegar
1 teaspoon sugar
½ teaspoon smoked paprika
½ teaspoon salt
½ teaspoon freshly ground black pepper
¼ teaspoon garlic powder
⅛ teaspoon red pepper flakes

1. Remove the core from the cabbage. Cut the cabbage in half and then into quarters. Cut the quarters into smaller uniform wedges to ensure even cooking.

2. Preheat the air fryer to 400°F.

3. In a small bowl, combine the olive oil, vinegar, sugar, paprika, salt, pepper, garlic powder, and red pepper flakes.

4. In a large bowl, toss the cabbage pieces with the oil mixture until well coated.

5. Lightly spray the air fryer basket with oil. Place the coated cabbage wedges in the basket.

6. Air fry for 8 minutes. Flip the cabbage wedges and lightly spray with oil. Air fry for an additional 6 minutes, or until tender and lightly browned.

PER SERVING: Calories: 124; Total fat: 7g; Saturated fat: 1g; Cholesterol: 0mg; Sodium: 337mg; Carbohydrates: 15g; Fiber: 5g; Protein: 3g

Veggie-Stuffed Peppers

Veggie-Stuffed Peppers make a delightful meat-free meal that is both filling and nutritious. With salsa, beans, rice, and cheese, plus spices and meaty mushrooms, they are full of flavor and turn out perfectly with only 10 minutes in the air fryer.

GLUTEN-FREE, VEGETARIAN, 30 MINUTES OR LESS

PREP TIME: 10 minutes
COOK TIME: 10 minutes
SERVES 4
TEMPERATURE: 360°F

4 medium bell peppers
1 (15-ounce) can black beans, drained and rinsed
1½ cups cooked white rice
1 cup shredded cheddar cheese
1 cup salsa
½ cup diced mushrooms
1¼ teaspoons chili powder
1 teaspoon salt
½ teaspoon freshly ground black pepper
½ teaspoon ground cumin
Extra-virgin olive oil, for the basket

1. Cut ½ inch off the top of the bell peppers, and then cut them in half lengthwise. Remove and discard the seeds and set aside the peppers.

2. In a large bowl, combine the black beans, rice, cheese, salsa, mushrooms, chili powder, salt, pepper, and cumin.

3. Preheat the air fryer to 360°F.

4. Spoon the bean mixture into the pepper halves.

5. Lightly spray the air fryer basket with oil. Place the stuffed pepper halves in the basket. (Air fry in batches, if necessary.)

6. Air fry for 10 minutes, or until the peppers begin to soften.

Air Frying Tip: If you are using green bell peppers, air fry for 12 minutes. Green bell peppers are firmer than red, yellow, or orange varieties and take a little longer to get tender.

PER SERVING: Calories: 352; Total fat: 11g; Saturated fat: 6g; Cholesterol: 28mg; Sodium: 1,555mg; Carbohydrates: 50g; Fiber: 12g; Protein: 17g

Tofu and Broccoli Bowls

Tofu and Broccoli Bowls are a delicious and vegan-friendly meal for lunch or dinner. The tofu turns out nice and crispy in the air fryer in only minutes. The result is balanced nutrition in a quick and easy one-bowl vegetarian meal.

DAIRY-FREE, GLUTEN-FREE, VEGAN

PREP TIME: 5 minutes, plus 30 minutes to marinate
COOK TIME: 25 minutes
SERVES 4
TEMPERATURE: 380°F

¼ cup soy sauce
1 tablespoon sesame oil
1 tablespoon brown sugar
1 tablespoon rice vinegar
1 tablespoon cornstarch
½ tablespoon grated fresh ginger
2 teaspoons minced garlic
½ teaspoon sriracha
1 (16-ounce) package extra-firm tofu, cut into ½-inch cubes
Extra-virgin olive oil, for spraying
1 medium head broccoli, florets cut into bite-size pieces
½ teaspoon salt
½ teaspoon freshly ground black pepper
2 cups cooked white rice, for serving

1. In a small bowl, combine the soy sauce, sesame oil, brown sugar, rice vinegar, cornstarch, ginger, garlic, and sriracha.

2. Put the tofu cubes in a large zip-top bag. Coat the tofu with the marinade, seal the bag, and refrigerate for 30 minutes.

3. Preheat the air fryer to 380°F.

4. Lightly spray the air fryer basket with oil. Place the tofu in the basket and lightly spray with oil.

5. Air fry for 5 minutes. Carefully flip the tofu cubes and lightly spray with oil. Air fry for an additional 5 minutes.

6. While the tofu is air frying, season the broccoli florets with the salt and pepper.

7. Remove the tofu from the air fryer basket, transfer to a medium bowl, and put the broccoli florets in the basket. Lightly spray with oil.

8. Air fry for 15 minutes, shaking the basket and lightly spraying with oil every 5 minutes, until the broccoli is tender and slightly roasted.

9. Serve over a bowl of white rice.

PER SERVING: Calories: 350; Total fat: 12g; Saturated fat: 2g; Cholesterol: 0mg; Sodium: 1,230mg; Carbohydrates: 42g; Fiber: 6g; Protein: 20g

Feta-Stuffed Tomatoes

The bold Greek flavors of tomato, feta cheese, and spices make this dish marvelous. It's perfect for summer, when gardens are overflowing with tomatoes and you don't want to heat up your house by turning on the oven.

30 MINUTES OR LESS

PREP TIME: 15 minutes
COOK TIME: 10 minutes
SERVES 4
TEMPERATURE: 370°F

4 large ripe but firm
    tomatoes
4 ounces crumbled
    feta cheese
½ cup Italian bread crumbs
2 tablespoons chopped
    roasted red bell peppers
    (from a jar), drained
2 tablespoons chopped
    fresh parsley
2 tablespoons extra-virgin
    olive oil, plus more for
    the basket
½ teaspoon salt
½ teaspoon freshly ground
    black pepper
Pinch cayenne pepper

1. Cut the tomatoes in half horizontally. Scoop the pulp out of each tomato half with a spoon, leaving the shells intact.

2. Discard the seeds and chop the tomato pulp coarsely.

3. In a medium bowl, combine the tomato pulp, cheese, bread crumbs, roasted red peppers, parsley, olive oil, salt, black pepper, and cayenne pepper.

4. Preheat the air fryer to 370°F.

5. Spoon the mixture evenly into the tomato shells.

6. Lightly spray the air fryer basket with oil. Place the stuffed tomato halves in the basket.

7. Air fry for 10 minutes, or until the tomatoes are tender.

PER SERVING: Calories: 225; Total fat: 14g; Saturated fat: 5g; Cholesterol: 25mg; Sodium: 833mg; Carbohydrates: 18g; Fiber: 3g; Protein: 8g

Margherita Portobello Pizza

Large portobello mushroom caps make a wonderful pizza crust. The traditional flavors of margherita pizza go perfectly with the earthy mushrooms to create a delightful meat-free meal.

GLUTEN-FREE, VEGETARIAN,
30 MINUTES OR LESS

PREP TIME: 5 minutes
COOK TIME: 10 minutes
SERVES 4
TEMPERATURE: 400°F

4 large portobello
   mushrooms, stems
   removed and
   thoroughly cleaned
Extra-virgin olive oil, for
   spraying
½ teaspoon salt
½ teaspoon freshly ground
   black pepper
½ cup marinara sauce
¼ cup fresh basil leaves
½ cup cherry
   tomatoes, sliced
4 ounces fresh
   mozzarella, sliced
2 tablespoons
   balsamic vinegar

1. Use a spoon to gently scrape off the gills on the inside of the mushroom caps.

2. Spray the caps with olive oil on both sides and season with the salt and pepper.

3. Preheat the air fryer to 400°F.

4. Lightly spray the air fryer basket with oil. Place the mushrooms gill-side down in the basket. (Air fry in batches, if necessary.)

5. Air fry for 4 minutes. Flip the mushrooms and lightly spray with oil. Air fry for an additional 3 minutes.

6. Open the air fryer and spoon 2 tablespoons marinara sauce onto each mushroom. Top with the basil, tomatoes, and cheese. Press the toppings into the marinara sauce to prevent them from flying around in the air fryer.

7. Air fry for an additional 3 to 4 minutes, or until the cheese has melted and is lightly browned.

8. Drizzle balsamic vinegar over the top and serve.

PER SERVING: Calories: 135; Total fat: 8g; Saturated fat: 4g; Cholesterol: 25mg; Sodium: 535mg; Carbohydrates: 10g; Fiber: 2g; Protein: 7g

Veggie Burgers

Veggie burgers are a modern classic and a wonderful meatless meal. Chickpeas provide a great source of protein, the zucchini adds moisture, and the spices infuse the burger with flavor. The air fryer gets them nice and crispy.

VEGETARIAN

PREP TIME: 10 minutes, plus 1 hour 30 minutes to chill
COOK TIME: 10 minutes
SERVES 4
TEMPERATURE: 370°F

1 (15-ounce) can chickpeas, drained and rinsed
1 small zucchini
¼ cup plain bread crumbs
1 tablespoon minced garlic
1 teaspoon paprika
1 teaspoon onion powder
1 teaspoon salt
½ teaspoon freshly ground black pepper
½ teaspoon ground cumin
½ teaspoon garlic powder
Extra-virgin olive oil, for spraying
4 hamburger buns, for serving
Lettuce, tomato, and onion, for topping (optional)

1. In a large bowl, mash the chickpeas with a potato masher until hardly any chunks remain.

2. Peel the zucchini and grate it onto a clean kitchen towel. Squeeze out as much moisture as possible.

3. Add the zucchini, bread crumbs, garlic, paprika, onion powder, salt, pepper, cumin, and garlic powder to the chickpeas. Mix the ingredients until they form a thick dough. Refrigerate for 1 hour.

4. Wet your hands and divide the dough into four parts. Form the dough into equal-size patties. If the dough is too sticky, add 1 to 2 tablespoons bread crumbs. Refrigerate the patties for an additional 30 minutes.

5. Preheat the air fryer to 370°F.

6. Lightly spray the air fryer basket with oil. Place the veggie patties in a single layer in the basket. (Air fry in batches, if necessary.) Lightly spray with oil.

7. Air fry for 6 minutes. Flip the veggie patties and lightly spray with oil. Air fry for another 6 minutes.

8. Serve on hamburger buns with your desired toppings.

Variation: For a vegan meal, serve on large lettuce leaves.

PER SERVING: Calories: 254; Total fat: 4g; Saturated fat: 1g; Cholesterol: 0mg; Sodium: 996mg; Carbohydrates: 44g; Fiber: 6g; Protein: 10g

Baked Sweet Potatoes

Baked sweet potatoes in the air fryer come out with a soft, fluffy center and a nice crispy exterior. These make for a simple yet delicious side dish that tastes amazing topped with butter and a little cinnamon and sugar. Or make them savory and serve like you would your ideal baked white potato. Sweet potatoes bring extra nutrients to the table.

DAIRY-FREE, GLUTEN-FREE, VEGAN

PREP TIME: 5 minutes
COOK TIME: 50 minutes
SERVES 4
TEMPERATURE: 390°F

4 medium sweet potatoes
Extra-virgin olive oil, for spraying
1 to 2 teaspoons salt
½ teaspoon freshly ground black pepper

1. Preheat the air fryer to 390°F.

2. Pierce the sweet potatoes several times with a fork or knife.

3. Spray olive oil all over the sweet potatoes and season with salt and pepper to taste.

4. Lightly spray the air fryer basket with oil. Place the sweet potatoes in a single layer in the basket, leaving ½ inch between each to ensure even cooking. (Air fry in batches, if necessary.)

5. Air fry for 20 minutes. Flip the sweet potatoes and air fry for an additional 20 to 30 minutes, or until fork-tender.

Air Frying Tip: The cook time will depend on the size of the sweet potatoes. Pick sweet potatoes that are long and skinny because they will cook more evenly than larger bulbous sweet potatoes. Be sure the potatoes are dry before air frying, so they air fry instead of steam.

PER SERVING: Calories: 113; Total fat: <1g; Saturated fat: 0g; Cholesterol: 0mg; Sodium: 661mg; Carbohydrates: 26g; Fiber: 4g; Protein: 2g

CHAPTER 9

Desserts, Snacks, and Breads

Candied Pecans

Candied pecans are a great snack. Roasting the nuts really brings out a richness of flavor that pairs perfectly with a touch of sweetness. Put these sweet, crunchy nuts in a pretty jar and add a ribbon for a wonderful gift for friends or family during the holidays.

DAIRY-FREE, GLUTEN-FREE, VEGETARIAN, 30 MINUTES OR LESS

PREP TIME: 5 minutes
COOK TIME: 15 minutes, plus 10 minutes to cool
SERVES 4
TEMPERATURE: 300°F

1 large egg white
1 tablespoon water
1 teaspoon vanilla extract
8 ounces pecan halves
¼ cup granulated sugar
¼ cup light brown sugar
½ teaspoon pumpkin pie spice
⅛ teaspoon salt
Extra-virgin olive oil, for the basket

1. Preheat the air fryer to 300°F.

2. In a medium bowl, whisk the egg white, water, and vanilla until the egg white is frothy.

3. Add the pecans and stir to coat.

4. Add the granulated sugar, brown sugar, pumpkin pie spice, and salt to the coated pecans and stir until the pecans are covered.

5. Lightly spray the air fryer basket with oil. Place the pecans in the basket.

6. Air fry for 15 minutes, shaking the basket every 5 minutes.

7. Transfer the pecans to a sheet of parchment paper to cool for 10 minutes. The candy coating will harden during the cooling period.

8. Store any leftovers in an airtight container for up to 2 weeks.

Air Frying Tip: The fryer basket will be very sticky and should be soaked or washed promptly.

Variation: If you don't have pumpkin pie spice on hand you can substitute cinnamon.

PER SERVING: Calories: 488; Total fat: 42g; Saturated fat: 4g; Cholesterol: 0mg; Sodium: 56mg; Carbohydrates: 29g; Fiber: 6g; Protein: 7g

Cinnamon and Sugar Chickpeas

You may have tried savory crispy chickpeas, but their mild flavor also makes them perfect for a sweet snack. They crisp up perfectly in the air fryer for a protein-packed dessert that's easy, affordable, and ready to eat in only 15 minutes.

DAIRY-FREE, GLUTEN-FREE,
VEGAN, 30 MINUTES OR LESS

PREP TIME: 5 minutes
COOK TIME: 15 minutes
SERVES 4
TEMPERATURE: 390°F

1 tablespoon ground
   cinnamon
½ cup sugar
1 (15-ounce) can chickpeas,
   drained and rinsed
Extra-virgin olive oil, for
   the basket

1. Preheat the air fryer to 390°F.

2. In a medium bowl, combine the cinnamon and sugar. Add the chickpeas and stir to coat.

3. Lightly spray the air fryer basket with oil. Place the coated chickpeas in the basket.

4. Air fry for 15 minutes, shaking the fryer basket every 5 minutes.

5. Remove the chickpeas from the basket immediately.

6. Store any leftovers in an airtight container for up to 3 days.

Air Frying Tip: The fryer basket will be very sticky and should be washed or soaked promptly.

PER SERVING: Calories: 194; Total fat: 2g; Saturated fat: <1g; Cholesterol: 0mg; Sodium: 141mg; Carbohydrates: 42g; Fiber: 5g; Protein: 5g

Twisted Parmesan Breadsticks

Puff pastry breadsticks are incredibly easy to prepare, in addition to being light in texture and delicious to eat. The blend of spices and Parmesan cheese makes these a treat on their own, as an appetizer, or as an addition to any meal.

30 MINUTES OR LESS

PREP TIME: 10 minutes
COOK TIME: 10 minutes
SERVES 5
TEMPERATURE: 350°F

1 sheet puff pastry, at room
    temperature
1 large egg
1 tablespoon water
½ cup grated
    Parmesan cheese
1 teaspoon paprika
⅛ teaspoon cayenne pepper
Extra-virgin olive oil, for
    greasing the basket

1. Preheat the air fryer to 350°F.

2. Roll out the sheet of puff pastry until it is about ⅛ inch thick.

3. In a small bowl, whisk together the egg and water to make an egg wash. Using a pastry brush, brush the pastry with the egg wash.

4. Sprinkle the Parmesan cheese, paprika, and cayenne pepper over the surface of the pastry. Press on the cheese and spices to ensure they adhere.

5. Use a knife or pizza cutter to cut the pastry into strips about ½ inch wide. Twist each strip.

6. Lightly spray the air fryer basket with oil. Place the twisted breadsticks in the basket, leaving 1 inch between each to ensure even cooking. (Air fry in batches, if necessary.)

7. Air fry for 10 minutes, shaking the basket after 5 minutes.

8. Serve warm.

Air Frying Tip: If you have a small air fryer basket you can cut the pastry into shorter strips. The cook time should remain the same.

PER SERVING: Calories: 419; Total fat: 28g; Saturated fat: 14g; Cholesterol: 46mg; Sodium: 529mg; Carbohydrates: 33g; Fiber: 1g; Protein: 9g

Fresh Berry Wonton Cups

A crisp wonton cup is a great complement to the sweetness and tartness of the berry mixture in this handheld dessert. Enjoy this wonderful treat any time of year, but especially in the summer, when berries are in season.

VEGETARIAN, 30 MINUTES OR LESS

PREP TIME: 10 minutes
COOK TIME: 10 minutes, plus 10 minutes to cool
SERVES 6
TEMPERATURE: 350°F

12 wonton wrappers
Extra-virgin olive oil, for spraying
4 teaspoons granulated sugar, divided
½ teaspoon ground cinnamon, divided
¼ cup raspberry preserves
1 cup fresh blueberries
1 cup fresh raspberries
1 teaspoon freshly squeezed lemon juice

1. Preheat the air fryer to 350°F.

2. Press one wonton wrapper into a silicone muffin cup. Repeat until you have filled 12 muffin cups. The wrappers should resemble small cups. Lightly spray the wrappers with oil.

3. In a small bowl, combine 3 teaspoons sugar and ¼ teaspoon cinnamon. Sprinkle the mixture onto each wrapper. Place the muffin cups in the air fryer basket.

4. Air fry for 6 to 8 minutes, or until the wrappers are lightly browned and crispy. Let the wrappers cool for 10 minutes.

5. While the wonton cups are cooling, put the raspberry preserves in a medium bowl and microwave for 30 seconds to 1 minute, or until soft.

6. Add the blueberries, raspberries, and lemon juice, along with the remaining 1 teaspoon sugar and ¼ teaspoon cinnamon, to the bowl of preserves and stir to coat all the berries.

7. Spoon the berry mixture into the wonton cups and serve.

Variation: You can use any berries you have on hand for this recipe. Just make sure you have about 2 cups.

PER SERVING: Calories: 116; Total fat: 1g; Saturated fat: <1g; Cholesterol: 1mg; Sodium: 92mg; Carbohydrates: 27g; Fiber: 2g; Protein: 2g

Blueberry Hand Pies

These small pies highlight the taste of fresh blueberries. The crust turns golden brown and crispy and is topped with just a hint of sugar, creating a perfect individual dessert for a day at the park (or at home!).

VEGETARIAN, 30 MINUTES OR LESS

PREP TIME: 15 minutes
COOK TIME: 10 minutes
SERVES 6
TEMPERATURE: 350°F

1 box refrigerated piecrusts (2 crusts)
1 pint blueberries
2 tablespoons cornstarch
1 tablespoon freshly squeezed lemon juice
⅓ cup granulated sugar, plus more for sprinkling
Pinch salt
1 large egg
1 tablespoon water
Extra-virgin olive oil, for the parchment paper

1. Preheat the air fryer to 350°F.

2. Unroll the piecrusts. Using a large cookie cutter or the mouth of a jar that is 4 to 5 inches in diameter, cut circles out of dough. Gather the scraps, roll them out, and continue cutting circles. You should have about 12 circles of dough.

3. In a medium bowl, combine the blueberries, cornstarch, lemon juice, sugar, and salt.

4. In a small bowl, whisk the egg and water together to make an egg wash.

5. Place 1 tablespoon of blueberry mixture in the center of each dough circle. Fold the dough over the filling so it makes a half-moon shape. Press the edges of the dough together to seal and use a fork to crimp the edges.

6. Brush the tops of the hand pies with the egg wash and sprinkle with sugar.

7. Place a sheet of air fryer parchment paper in the basket. Lightly spray the parchment with oil. Place the hand pies in a single layer in the basket, leaving ½ inch of space between each to ensure even cooking. (Air fry in batches, if necessary.)

8. Air fry for 8 to 10 minutes, or until golden brown and completely cooked.

9. Serve warm or cool. Store in an airtight container for up to 3 days.

Air Frying Tip: The pie dough will tend to stick to the fryer basket if you do not use parchment paper. If you prefer not to use parchment paper, be sure to loosen the pies after they cook for 4 minutes and spray the basket liberally with olive oil.

Variation: You can use fresh berries of your choice for this recipe.

PER SERVING: Calories: 434; Total fat: 21g; Saturated fat: 8g; Cholesterol: 31mg; Sodium: 323mg; Carbohydrates: 60g; Fiber: 3g; Protein: 4g

Cheesy Garlic Bread

This Cheesy Garlic Bread is such a wonderful treat and the perfect side to almost any dinner, from Spicy Italian Zucchini Boats (page 188) to Veggie-Stuffed Peppers (page 199). It is also great eaten alone with some marinara sauce as a snack. If you love crispy, crunchy garlic bread, this will be your go-to recipe.

VEGETARIAN, 30 MINUTES OR LESS

PREP TIME: 10 minutes
COOK TIME: 5 minutes
SERVES 6
TEMPERATURE: 400°F

1 baguette
½ cup unsalted butter, at room temperature
1 teaspoon garlic powder
Freshly ground black pepper
1 cup shredded cheddar cheese
Extra-virgin olive oil, for greasing the basket
Fresh parsley, chopped (optional)

1. Preheat the air fryer to 400°F.

2. Cut the baguette in half lengthwise, then cut each half into thirds.

3. Spread the butter on the inside of each piece of bread. Sprinkle garlic powder on each piece and season with pepper.

4. Sprinkle cheese on top of each piece of bread. Press on the cheese to ensure it adheres.

5. Lightly spray the air fryer basket with oil. Place the bread in a single layer in the basket. (Air fry in batches, if necessary.)

6. Air fry for 3 to 5 minutes, or until the cheese has melted and the bread is crisp.

7. Garnish with fresh chopped parsley, if using. Serve warm.

Variation: Any variety of shredded cheese will work for this recipe.

PER SERVING: Calories: 282; Total fat: 22g; Saturated fat: 13g; Cholesterol: 59mg; Sodium: 397mg; Carbohydrates: 14g; Fiber: 1g; Protein: 7g

Honey-Lime Pineapple Skewers

The flavors of honey, lime, and caramelized pineapple blend together for a heavenly island-themed dessert that is simple and almost too good to be true. Avoid canned pineapple: fresh is a must for this recipe!

DAIRY-FREE, GLUTEN-FREE, VEGAN, 30 MINUTES OR LESS

PREP TIME: 15 minutes
COOK TIME: 10 minutes
SERVES 4
TEMPERATURE: 400°F

1 small pineapple, peeled, cored, and cut into 2-inch chunks
¼ cup honey
2 tablespoons freshly squeezed lime juice
Extra-virgin olive oil, for the basket

1. Preheat the air fryer to 400°F.

2. Thread the pineapple chunks onto 6-inch metal skewers.

3. In a small bowl, whisk together the honey and lime juice.

4. Brush the pineapple with the honey-lime marinade.

5. Lightly spray the air fryer basket with oil. Place the pineapple skewers in a single layer in the basket.

6. Air fry for 6 to 8 minutes, flipping the skewers over after 4 minutes, until the pineapple is heated through and the honey is caramelized.

Air Frying Tip: Many air fryer accessory kits contain 6-inch metal skewers and a grilling rack that the skewers sit on. They work great for all kinds of kebab recipes.

PER SERVING: Calories: 179; Total fat: <1g; Saturated fat: 0g; Cholesterol: 0mg; Sodium: 3mg; Carbohydrates: 48g; Fiber: 3g; Protein: 1g

Plantain Chips

Plantains are too fibrous to be eaten raw, but they are excellent when fried. They are eaten in many countries across the world, from Africa to South America. Eating air-fried plantain chips is guilt-free snacking at its best. Using overly ripe plantains produces a sweet chip that is perfect for a healthy treat.

DAIRY-FREE, GLUTEN-FREE, VEGAN, 30 MINUTES OR LESS

PREP TIME: 5 minutes
COOK TIME: 15 minutes
SERVES 4
TEMPERATURE: 350°F

2 overly ripe yellow plantains (peel should be black)
Extra-virgin olive oil, for spraying
Sea salt (optional)

1. Preheat the air fryer to 350°F.

2. Peel the plantains and discard the peels. Cut the plantains into ½-inch-thick slices.

3. Lightly spray the air fryer basket with oil. Place the plantains in a single layer in the basket. Lightly spray with oil.

4. Air fry for 10 minutes. Flip the plantains and lightly spray with oil. Air fry for an additional 5 to 7 minutes, or until browned, crispy, and caramelized.

5. Sprinkle sea salt over the plantains, if using, and serve.

Air Frying Tip: Thinner plantain slices will cook more quickly and should be watched closely during the last few minutes to prevent overcooking.

PER SERVING: Calories: 165; Total fat: 1g; Saturated fat: 0g; Cholesterol: 0mg; Sodium: 5mg; Carbohydrates: 43g; Fiber: 2g; Protein: 2g

Apple Fries

Baked apple fries are a healthy sweet treat that is sure to become a family favorite. They are wonderful on their own, or you can serve them with a side of caramel sauce or a dusting of confectioners' sugar.

DAIRY-FREE, VEGETARIAN, 30 MINUTES OR LESS

PREP TIME: 15 minutes
COOK TIME: 10 minutes
SERVES 4 TO 6
TEMPERATURE: 350°F

½ cup cornstarch
2 teaspoons ground
  cinnamon
4 Granny Smith apples,
  peeled, cored, and sliced
  into 8 wedges
2 large eggs
1 cup graham
  cracker crumbs
¼ cup packed light
  brown sugar
Extra-virgin olive oil or
  avocado oil, for spraying

1. In a small bowl, combine the cornstarch and cinnamon.

2. Place the apple wedges in a large zip-top bag. Pour in the cornstarch mixture, seal the bag, and shake it to coat the apples.

3. In a small shallow bowl, beat the eggs.

4. In a second small shallow bowl, combine the graham cracker crumbs and brown sugar.

5. Coat the cornstarch-covered apples in the egg, then in the graham crackers.

6. Preheat the air fryer to 350°F.

7. Lightly spray the air fryer basket with oil. Place the coated apple wedges in a single layer in the basket. Lightly spray with oil.

8. Air fry for 8 minutes. Flip the apples and lightly spray with oil. Air fry for an additional 2 to 3 minutes, or until the coating is crispy.

PER SERVING: Calories: 336; Total fat: 5g; Saturated fat: 1g; Cholesterol: 82mg; Sodium: 143mg; Carbohydrates: 71g; Fiber: 6g; Protein: 5g

Hush Puppies

Hush puppies are round savory balls made from a cornmeal-based batter. They are traditionally deep-fried and served in the American South as an accompaniment to seafood. Making hush puppies in the air fryer is simple and they turn out nice and crispy. Serve with Cod Nuggets (page 169) or Fried Catfish (page 160).

VEGETARIAN, 30 MINUTES OR LESS

PREP TIME: 10 minutes
COOK TIME: 10 minutes
SERVES 4
TEMPERATURE: 380°F

1 cup yellow cornmeal
¾ cup all-purpose flour
1½ teaspoons baking powder
½ teaspoon salt
¼ teaspoon garlic powder
⅛ teaspoon cayenne pepper
¼ cup onion, finely chopped
1 large egg
¾ cup milk
Extra-virgin olive oil, for spraying

1. In a medium bowl, combine the cornmeal, flour, baking powder, salt, garlic powder, and cayenne pepper. Mix in the onion, then whisk in the egg and milk. Let the batter rest for 5 minutes.

2. Preheat the air fryer to 380°F.

3. Generously spray the air fryer basket with oil. Use a 1-inch cookie scoop to form small balls of dough. Place the dough balls in a single layer in the basket. Lightly spray with oil.

4. Air fry for 5 minutes. Flip the hush puppies and lightly spray with oil. Air fry for an additional 5 minutes, or until crispy and golden brown.

PER SERVING: Calories: 247; Total fat: 4g; Saturated fat: 1g; Cholesterol: 46mg; Sodium: 523mg; Carbohydrates: 45g; Fiber: 3g; Protein: 8g

Cheesecake Chimichangas

The combination of cheesecake and warm tortillas is a dessert-lover's dream: sweet cream cheese filling inside a crispy tortilla coated in cinnamon and sugar. It's reminiscent of a filled churro, but without all the extra oil.

VEGETARIAN, 30 MINUTES OR LESS

PREP TIME: 15 minutes
COOK TIME: 10 minutes
SERVES 4
TEMPERATURE: 360°F

8 ounces cream cheese, softened
2 tablespoons granulated sugar, plus ¼ cup
½ tablespoon sour cream
¼ teaspoon vanilla extract
8 (6-inch) flour tortillas
1 teaspoon ground cinnamon
Extra-virgin olive oil, for spraying

1. In a medium bowl, beat the cream cheese with an electric mixer until it is smooth. Add 2 tablespoons sugar, the sour cream, and vanilla and mix well.

2. Place 2 tablespoons of the cream cheese mixture on the bottom portion of each flour tortilla. Fold in the sides of the tortilla and roll it up like an egg roll.

3. Preheat the air fryer to 360°F.

4. In a small shallow bowl, combine the remaining ¼ cup sugar and the cinnamon.

5. Lightly spray the air fryer basket with oil. Place the chimichangas in a single layer in the basket, leaving 1 inch of space between each to ensure even cooking. Lightly spray with oil.

6. Air fry for 4 minutes. Flip the chimichangas and lightly spray with oil. Air fry for an additional 4 minutes, or until golden brown.

7. Immediately roll the chimichangas in the cinnamon-sugar mixture and serve.

Variation: You can drizzle honey on top or serve with whipped topping.

PER SERVING: Calories: 477; Total fat: 25g; Saturated fat: 14g; Cholesterol: 58mg; Sodium: 719mg; Carbohydrates: 55g; Fiber: 4g; Protein: 10g

Easy Biscuits

There is quite simply nothing better than the taste of homemade biscuits. This recipe is straightforward, with only five ingredients. Biscuits can be served at breakfast, made into a sandwich, or served on the side with almost any meal. Always serve warm and brushed with melted butter.

VEGETARIAN

PREP TIME: 10 minutes, plus 15 minutes to chill
COOK TIME: 10 minutes
SERVES 4
TEMPERATURE: 400°F

2 cups self-rising flour, plus more for dusting
¼ teaspoon dried mustard
Pinch cayenne pepper
4 tablespoons salted butter, cut into small pieces
¾ cup milk
Extra-virgin olive oil, for the basket

1. In a medium bowl, combine the flour, dried mustard, and cayenne pepper.

2. Add the butter pieces to the bowl. Using a pastry cutter, lightly mix the butter into the flour and spices until it is pea-sized and well distributed.

3. Pour the milk into the flour mixture and use a large spoon to mix until it is combined and a soft dough begins to form. Do not overmix.

4. Dust your work surface with flour and place the dough on the floured surface. Flour your hands and gently knead the dough a few times until it is smooth.

5. Roll out the dough until it is about ¾ inch thick. Use a 2-inch biscuit cutter that has been dipped in flour to cut out the biscuits. You should have 8 biscuits.

6. Put the biscuits on a platter and refrigerate for 15 minutes.

7. Preheat the air fryer to 400°F.

8. Lightly spray the air fryer basket with oil. Place the biscuits in a single layer in the basket, leaving 1 inch of space between each to ensure even cooking.

9. Air fry for 10 minutes, or until golden brown on top and cooked through.

PER SERVING: Calories: 351; Total fat: 14g; Saturated fat: 8g; Cholesterol: 35mg; Sodium: 857mg; Carbohydrates: 49g; Fiber: 2g; Protein: 8g

Chocolate Lava Cake

Chocolate lava cake is a decadent treat that's so easy to make at home. These individual cakes are made in ramekins and fit perfectly in the air fryer. Serve to guests or make them as a special surprise for dessert during the week. Try them with a sprinkle of confectioners' sugar or a spoonful of whipped cream on top.

VEGETARIAN, 30 MINUTES OR LESS

PREP TIME: 10 minutes
COOK TIME: 10 minutes
SERVES 4
TEMPERATURE: 375°F

½ cup (1 stick) unsalted butter, at room temperature, plus more for greasing
1 tablespoon cocoa powder
4 ounces semisweet baking chocolate
1 cup confectioners' sugar
4 large eggs
6 tablespoons all-purpose flour
⅛ teaspoon salt

1. Preheat the air fryer to 375°F. Grease four small ramekins with butter, then dust with cocoa powder.

2. In a medium bowl, combine the ½ cup butter and chocolate. Place the bowl in the microwave and microwave for 1 minute, or until the butter is completely melted. Stir until the butter and chocolate are smooth. Stir in the sugar.

3. Add the eggs and beat for 1 minute.

4. Add the flour and salt and stir until just combined.

5. Spoon equal amounts of batter into each ramekin, then place the ramekins in the air fryer basket.

6. Air fry for 10 minutes, or until the sides of the cake are firm but the center is still soft.

7. Let the cakes rest for 2 minutes. Turn the ramekins upside down on plates to unmold. Serve immediately because the inside will continue to cook, and you will not get the lava effect if you eat the cake later.

PER SERVING: Calories: 569; Total fat: 37g; Saturated fat: 22g; Cholesterol: 225mg; Sodium: 277mg; Carbohydrates: 58g; Fiber: 4g; Protein: 9g

Brown Sugar Peach Halves

When peach season rolls around this dish will become your new favorite way to eat fresh peaches. The fruit ends up tender and juicy on the inside with a buttery, caramelized brown sugar top that is fantastic. Serve with ice cream or whipped cream.

VEGETARIAN, 30 MINUTES OR LESS

PREP TIME: 5 minutes
COOK TIME: 10 minutes
SERVES 4
TEMPERATURE: 380°F

2 fresh peaches
Extra-virgin olive oil, for the pan
1 tablespoon salted butter, at room temperature, divided
1 tablespoon light brown sugar
1 teaspoon pumpkin pie spice

1. Preheat the air fryer to 380°F.

2. Slice the peaches in half and remove the pits.

3. Lightly spray a small oven-safe pan that will fit in the air fryer with olive oil. Place the peaches in the pan.

4. Place ¼ tablespoon butter in the center of each peach half.

5. In a small bowl, combine the brown sugar and pumpkin pie spice. Sprinkle the mixture over the peach halves. Place the pan in the air fryer basket.

6. Air fry for 8 to 10 minutes, or until the peaches are tender and the top is caramelized and golden brown.

7. Serve warm.

PER SERVING: Calories: 64; Total fat: 3g; Saturated fat: 2g; Cholesterol: 8mg; Sodium: 24mg; Carbohydrates: 10g; Fiber: 1g; Protein: 1g

Savory Cheddar-Bacon Muffins

Savory muffins make a hearty breakfast, snack, or side to go along with dinner. The sharp cheddar and bacon really shine in these muffins, and that tiny hint of brown sugar adds a little twist to the overall flavor experience.

30 MINUTES OR LESS

PREP TIME: 10 minutes
COOK TIME: 10 minutes
SERVES 8
TEMPERATURE: 400°F

2 large eggs
2 cups all-purpose flour
¾ cup milk
⅓ cup vegetable oil
¼ cup light brown sugar
1 tablespoon baking powder
1 teaspoon onion powder
2 cups shredded sharp
  cheddar cheese
1 cup chopped
  cooked bacon

1. In a medium bowl, mix together the eggs, flour, milk, vegetable oil, brown sugar, baking powder, and onion powder until well combined. (It's okay if there are some small lumps.)

2. Stir in the cheese and bacon.

3. Preheat the air fryer to 400°F.

4. Fill 12 to 16 silicone muffin cups about half full of batter.

5. Place the muffin cups in a single layer in the air fryer basket. (Air fry in batches, if necessary.)

6. Air fry for 10 to 12 minutes, or until cooked through and golden brown on top.

7. Serve warm. Store leftovers in an airtight container for 3 to 4 days.

Air Frying Tip: You can check for doneness by inserting a toothpick into the center of the muffin. If it comes out clean, they should be cooked all the way through.

PER SERVING: Calories: 406; Total fat: 24g; Saturated fat: 9g; Cholesterol: 87mg; Sodium: 563mg; Carbohydrates: 31g; Fiber: 1g; Protein: 15g

Air Fryer Charts

FAVORITE FROZEN FOODS

FROZEN FOODS	QUANTITY	TIME	TEMP	NOTES
Breaded shrimp	Up to ½ pound	8 to 10 minutes	400°F	Spray with olive oil and flip halfway through cooking.
Chicken nuggets	6 to 12 pieces	10 to 15 minutes	400°F	Spray with olive oil and shake halfway through cooking.
Fish fillets	1 or 2 pieces	14 to 15 minutes	400°F	Spray with olive oil and flip halfway through cooking.
Fish sticks	6 to 12 pieces	6 to 10 minutes	400°F	Spray with olive oil and shake halfway through cooking.
Hash browns	1 or 2 pieces	15 to 18 minutes	370°F	Spray with olive oil and shake halfway through cooking.
Onion rings	½ pound	8 to 10 minutes	400°F	Spray with olive oil and flip halfway through cooking.
Tater tots	10 to 20 tots	10 to 12 minutes	400°F	Spray with olive oil and shake halfway through cooking.
Thick fries	10 to 20 fries	18 to 20 minutes	400°F	Spray with olive oil and shake halfway through cooking.
Thin fries	10 to 20 fries	14 minutes	400°F	Spray with olive oil and shake halfway through cooking.
Burgers	1 or 2 patties	14 to 15 minutes	400°F	Do not stack; flip halfway through cooking.
Burritos	1 or 2 burritos	8 to 10 minutes	400°F	Spray with olive oil and flip halfway through cooking.
Egg rolls	3 or 4 egg rolls	3 to 6 minutes	390°F	Brush or spray with oil before cooking.
Meatballs	5 to 10 meatballs	8 to 10 minutes	380°F	Flip halfway through cooking.
Mozzarella sticks	4 to 8 sticks	8 to 10 minutes	360°F	Spray with olive oil and flip halfway through cooking.
Pizza	½ pizza	5 to 10 minutes	390°F	Place pizza on parchment paper; make sure it fits in the basket.
Pizza bagels	2 or 3 pizza bagels	8 to 10 minutes	375°F	Spray with oil; do not stack.
Pizza rolls (bites)	5 to 10 pizza rolls	5 to 7 minutes	375°F	Spray with olive oil and shake halfway through cooking.
Pot stickers	5 to 10 pot stickers	8 to 10 minutes	400°F	Spray with olive oil and flip halfway through cooking.
Samosas	3 or 4 samosas	5 to 10 minutes	400°F	Spray with olive oil and shake halfway through cooking.

FRESH FOODS

FRESH VEGETABLES	QUANTITY	TIME	TEMP	NOTES
Asparagus	½ pound	5 to 8 minutes	400°F	Trim ends before cooking; spray with olive oil and sprinkle with seasonings.
Broccoli	1 to 2 cups	5 to 8 minutes	400°F	Spray with olive oil and sprinkle with seasonings.
Brussels sprouts	1 cup	13 to 15 minutes	380°F	Trim bottoms and cut in half before cooking; spray with olive oil and sprinkle with seasonings.
Carrots	½ to 1 cup	7 to 10 minutes	380°F	Cut first; spray with olive oil and sprinkle with seasonings.
Cauliflower florets	1 to 2 cups	9 to 10 minutes	360°F	Spray with olive oil and sprinkle with seasonings.
Corn on the cob	2 ears	6 minutes	390°F	Spray with olive oil and sprinkle with seasonings.
Eggplant	½ to 2 pounds	13 to 15 minutes	400°F	Cut into slices, spray with olive oil, and flip halfway through cooking.
Green beans	½ to 1 pound	5 minutes	400°F	Trim ends; spray with olive oil and shake halfway through cooking.
Kale	½ bunch	10 to 12 minutes	275°F	Trim leaves from the ribs; spray with olive oil and sprinkle with seasonings.
Mushrooms	½ to 1 cup	5 to 8 minutes	400°F	Trim stems first; sprinkle with seasonings.
Onions	½ to 1 pound	5 to 8 minutes	370°F	Cut first.
Peppers (bell)	½ to 1 cup	6 to 8 minutes	370°F	Cut first.
Potatoes (baked)	1 to 2 pounds	40 minutes	400°F	Poke holes first; spray with olive oil and sprinkle with seasonings.
Potatoes (cubed)	1 to 2 cups	15 minutes	400°F	Spray with olive oil and shake halfway through cooking.
Potatoes (fries)	1 to 2 cups	15 minutes	380°F	Spray with olive oil and shake halfway through cooking.
Potatoes (wedges)	1 to 3 cups	18 to 20 minutes	380°F	Spray with olive oil and shake halfway through cooking.
Squash	½ pound	12 to 13 minutes	400°F	Spray with olive oil and sprinkle with seasonings.
Sweet potatoes (baked)	1 large or 2 small sweet potatoes	35 to 40 minutes	390°F	Poke holes first; spray with olive oil and sprinkle with seasonings.
Sweet potatoes (cubed)	1 to 3 cups	14 to 20 minutes	380°F	Spray with olive oil and shake halfway through cooking.

FRESH VEGETABLES	QUANTITY	TIME	TEMP	NOTES
Sweet potatoes (fries)	1 to 2 cups	25 minutes	380°F	Spray with olive oil and shake halfway through cooking.
Tomatoes (breaded)	1 to 2 tomatoes	10 minutes	350°F	Cut first; season or bread and spray with oil.
Zucchini	½ to 1 pound	10 to 12 minutes	370°F	Cut first; spray with olive oil and sprinkle with seasonings.

CHICKEN	QUANTITY	TIME	TEMP	NOTES
Chicken breasts (boneless, skinless)	1 or 2 (6-ounce) breasts	12 to 15 minutes	380°F	Spray with olive oil; sprinkle with seasonings and flip halfway through cooking.
Chicken drumettes	Up to 4 drumettes	20 minutes	400°F	Spray with olive oil; sprinkle with seasonings and shake halfway through cooking.
Chicken drumsticks	1 to 4 drumsticks	16 to 20 minutes	390°F	Spray with olive oil; sprinkle with seasonings and shake halfway through cooking.
Chicken thighs (bone-in)	1 or 2 (6-ounce) thighs	22 minutes	380°F	Spray with olive oil; sprinkle with seasonings and flip halfway through cooking.
Chicken thighs (boneless)	1 or 2 (6-ounce) thighs	18 to 20 minutes	380°F	Spray with olive oil; sprinkle with seasonings and flip halfway through cooking.
Chicken tenders	Up to 4 tenders	8 to 10 minutes	375°F	Spray with olive oil; sprinkle with seasonings and shake halfway through cooking.
Chicken wings	Up to 4 wings	15 to 20 minutes	400°F	Spray with olive oil; sprinkle with seasonings and shake halfway through cooking.
Whole chicken	1 pound	75 minutes	360°F	Spray with olive oil; sprinkle with seasonings.

BEEF	QUANTITY	TIME	TEMP	NOTES
Burgers	1 or 2 patties	8 to 10 minutes	400°F	Do not stack; flip halfway through cooking.
Filet mignon	1 or 2 (6-ounce) steaks	8 to 10 minutes	360°F	Time will vary depending on your desired doneness; use a meat thermometer and cook to 125°F for rare, 135°F for medium-rare, 145°F for medium, 155°F for medium-well, and 160°F for well-done.
Flank steak	¼ to ½ pound	8 to 10 minutes	360°F	Time will vary depending on the desired doneness; use a meat thermometer and cook to 125°F for rare, 135°F for medium-rare, 145°F for medium, 155°F for medium-well, and 160°F for well-done.
Meatballs	5 to 10 meatballs	7 to 10 minutes	380°F	Sprinkle with seasonings and flip halfway through cooking.
Rib eye	1 or 2 (6-ounce) steaks	10 to 15 minutes	380°F	Time will vary depending on the desired doneness; use a meat thermometer and cook to 125°F for rare, 135°F for medium-rare, 145°F for medium, 155°F for medium-well, and 160°F for well-done.
Sirloin steak	1 or 2 (6-ounce) steaks	12 to 14 minutes	400°F	Time will vary depending on the desired doneness; use a meat thermometer and cook to 125°F for rare, 135°F for medium-rare, 145°F for medium, 155°F for medium-well, and 160°F for well-done.

PORK AND LAMB	QUANTITY	TIME	TEMP	NOTES
Bacon	2 to 4 slices	7 to 10 minutes	400°F	Flip halfway through cooking.
Lamb chops	1 or 2 (3-ounce) chops	10 to 12 minutes	400°F	Do not stack; sprinkle with seasonings and flip halfway through cooking.
Pork chops (bone-in or boneless)	1 or 2 (3-ounce) chops	12 to 15 minutes	380°F	Spray with olive oil; sprinkle with seasonings and flip halfway through cooking.
Pork loin	¼ to ½ pound	50 to 60 minutes	360°F	Spray with olive oil; sprinkle with seasonings and flip halfway through cooking.
Pork tenderloin	¼ to ½ pound	12 to 15 minutes	390°F	Spray with olive oil; sprinkle with seasonings and cook whole.
Rack of lamb	¼ to ½ pound	22 to 25 minutes	380°F	Do not stack; flip halfway through cooking.
Sausage (links)	5 to 10 links	13 to 15 minutes	380°F	Pierce holes in the sausage first.
Sausage (patties)	1 to 4 patties	13 to 15 minutes	380°F	Flip halfway through cooking.

FISH AND SEAFOOD	QUANTITY	TIME	TEMP	NOTES
Crab cakes	1 or 2 cakes	8 to 10 minutes	375°F	Toss with cornstarch; spray with olive oil and sprinkle with seasonings.
Fish fillets	¼ to ½ pound	10 to 12 minutes	320°F	Spray with olive oil and sprinkle with seasonings.
Scallops	¼ to ½ pound	5 to 7 minutes	320°F	Spray with olive oil and sprinkle with seasonings.
Shrimp	¼ to ½ pound	7 to 8 minutes	400°F	Peel and devein; spray with olive oil and sprinkle with seasonings.

FRESH FRUIT	QUANTITY	TIME	TEMP	NOTES
Apples	1 to 3 cups	4 to 7 minutes	350°F	Cut first; peel if desired.
Bananas	1 to 3 cups	4 to 7 minutes	350°F	Peel and cut first.
Peaches	1 to 3 cups	5 to 6 minutes	350°F	Cut first.

Measurement Conversions

	US STANDARD	US STANDARD (OUNCES)	METRIC (APPROXIMATE)
VOLUME EQUIVALENTS (LIQUID)	2 tablespoons	1 fl. oz.	30 mL
	¼ cup	2 fl. oz.	60 mL
	½ cup	4 fl. oz.	120 mL
	1 cup	8 fl. oz.	240 mL
	1½ cups	12 fl. oz.	355 mL
	2 cups or 1 pint	16 fl. oz.	475 mL
	4 cups or 1 quart	32 fl. oz.	1 L
	1 gallon	128 fl. oz.	4 L
VOLUME EQUIVALENTS (DRY)	⅛ teaspoon		0.5 mL
	¼ teaspoon		1 mL
	½ teaspoon		2 mL
	¾ teaspoon		4 mL
	1 teaspoon		5 mL
	1 tablespoon		15 mL
	¼ cup		59 mL
	⅓ cup		79 mL
	½ cup		118 mL
	⅔ cup		156 mL
	¾ cup		177 mL
	1 cup		235 mL
	2 cups or 1 pint		475 mL
	3 cups		700 mL
	4 cups or 1 quart		1 L
	½ gallon		2 L
	1 gallon		4 L
WEIGHT EQUIVALENTS	½ ounce		15 g
	1 ounce		30 g
	2 ounces		60 g
	4 ounces		115 g
	8 ounces		225 g
	12 ounces		340 g
	16 ounces or 1 pound		455 g

	FAHRENHEIT (F)	CELSIUS (C) (APPROXIMATE)
OVEN TEMPERATURES	250°F	120°C
	300°F	150°C
	325°F	180°C
	375°F	190°C
	400°F	200°C
	425°F	220°C
	450°F	230°C

Index

V

Acknowledgments

The book would not have been possible without the wisdom and support of other people in my life. I am not an island, and I have been blessed to be surrounded by many caring people.

I want to start by thanking my husband, Daniel. He is the first one to jump behind any idea or project I take on, with his full support. His consistent belief in my abilities has helped me try new things and make huge career changes. Thank you for being my best friend and someone I am proud to call my husband. I also appreciate your willingness to try any food I put in front of you.

My children deserve acknowledgment for their patience during the writing process. They were understanding of my high stress level, irritability, time limitations, and all those extra dirty dishes. Thanks for continuing to be honest recipe testers and, as always, the center of my world.

My parents, Terry and Linda Dick, taught me to work hard and follow through on my commitments. They also let me borrow their new air fryer so I could test more than one recipe at a time! My parents have assisted me in more ways than I can list, and I am grateful to have such constant support and love in my life.

A special thanks to Progna Ghosh, who has assisted me professionally and personally. Getting to know her has been an unexpected blessing. Although we have not met in person, she has impacted my life from afar. Her commitment to detail and follow-through is an example for others to follow.

I want to thank my Life is Sweeter by Design audience. The encouragement and support I get through messages, emails, and social media are what push me to continue forward on this blogging journey.

Lastly, I would like to thank Callisto Media for providing me with the amazing opportunity to write a second cookbook. My editor, Anne Lowrey, has been positive and helpful throughout this process and a pleasure to work alongside.

About the Author

Jamie Yonash is the creator of the websites Life is Sweeter by Design (LifeIsSweeterByDesign.com), Peace Love Christmas (PeaceLoveChristmas.com), and Find a Free Printable (FindAFreePrintable.com). She believes that you can design a sweet life with a little effort and a joyful attitude. Never wanting to add to the plate of busy moms, Jamie creates recipes, crafts, and tips that help parents achieve their own sweet life without added stress. Jamie's websites get more than 2 million visitors a year and many visitors stop by to find easy recipe ideas and more in a judgment-free zone!

Jamie is a lifelong resident of Kansas and loves small-town life. After graduating from high school, she pursued a nursing degree and graduated from Southwestern College in Winfield, Kansas, with a Bachelor of Science in Nursing. She worked as a nurse for more than 20 years before resigning to pursue her online business full time. Jamie has known her husband since she was 5 years old. She knew on their first date at the age of 22 that he was the man she was going to marry. Four children later, they continue to work hard to appreciate the sweetness of every-day life.

CPSIA information can be obtained
at www.ICGtesting.com
Printed in the USA
JSHW011112281121
20824JS00002B/3

9 781648 767449